3OO PLUS

VOLLEYBALL

DRILLS AND IDEAS

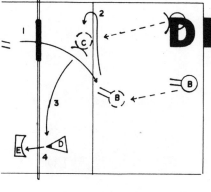

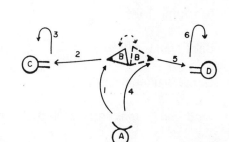
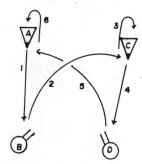
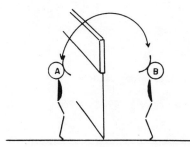
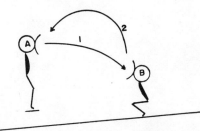

ROBERT D. BRATTON

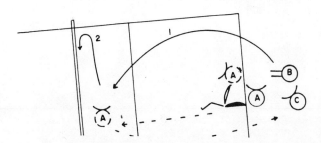

©CANADIAN VOLLEYBALL ASSOCIATION

333 River Road

Ottawa, Ontario

K1L 8B9

TABLE OF CONTENTS

Preface

The Author

CANADIAN VOLLEYBALL ASSOCIATION
333 River Road, Vanier, Ontario
CANADA K1L 8B9

Fifth Printing — November 1978
ISBN 0-920412-08-4

Printed in Canada
by
Dollco Printing Limited

PREFACE

300 Plus Volleyball Drills and Ideas was prepared in response to a need that had been expressed by numerous coaches, teachers, and students. They wanted an extensive resource file that would be clear and easy to use. The author and the Canadian Volleyball Association hope that we have succeeded in serving that need.

The drills and ideas have been accumulated from a variety of sources over the 18 years that the author has been associated with volleyball. Many of the drills and ideas are original. Most have been gathered from other sources as a result of interaction with many teachers, coaches, players, and students. There are drills from Japanese, Soviet, German, French, Canadian and United States sources.

Some of the drills are designed for the beginner and young child. Others are suited only for top calibre players. The coach will have to select those drills and ideas that are appropriate for his or her players. The drills in each chapter are more or less arranged in a sequence starting with very basic and moving through to some rather difficult drills. Each has been both explained and illustrated to facilitate clearer understanding.

The first four chapters present passing drills starting with one player and moving through to four or more players. Chapter Five includes drills for serving and receiving. Chapter Six offers a number of spiking drills and Chapter Seven presents blocking drills. Chapter Eight deals with back court defensive skills such as digging, diving, and rolling.

The last two chapters are rather unique. A number of drills have been presented in Chapter Nine that allow one player to practice a sequence of skills as he might experience them in a game. These drills are fairly comprehensive and should be of benefit to many senior teams. Chapter Ten includes a number of games and ideas that are designed to increase motivation and interest for students and players.

I would like to acknowledge the direct and indirect contributions from Kit Lefroy, Vic Lindal, Val Keller, Duane Tritter, John Gay and Mike Farnawani. I would also like to thank the many students and players who have influenced my thoughts over the years. Most of all I want to thank Marilyn, Greg, Rod and Tanice for helping me in every way.

THE AUTHOR

Bob Bratton is currently Associate Professor of Physical Education at the University of Calgary specializing in volleyball and sport sociology. He was born and raised in Winnipeg and attended the University of Manitoba. He received his B.Sc. from George Williams College in Chicago, his M.Sc. from UCLA and a Ph.D. from the University of Illinois. He has also studied at the Sportchochschule in Koln, Germany.

He has played volleyball competitively for 15 years and has played in a number of U.S. and Canadian championships. His coaching background includes high school, junior, senior and University teams. He has coached both men and women. His University of Calgary team toured Europe in 1972. He has taught and coached volleyball at the University of Calgary since 1961. He has attended and conducted numerous local, regional and national clinics in various parts of Canada.

Dr. Bratton has held a large number of executive and committee positions with both the Alberta and Canadian Volleyball Associations. He is currently chairman of the Documentation Committee and a member of the Coaches Development Committee of the CVA. He is a national referee with international experience.

He is author of **Power Volleyball for Player, Teacher and Coach,** the first volleyball text to be published in Canada. He is co-author, with Kit Lefroy, of **Basic Volleyball Skills,** a text that was commissioned by the Federal Government through CAHPER. His historical research led to the publication of **Canadian Volleyball, A History to 1967.** His dissertation was a sociological study of Canadian sports associations and included a study of the Canadian Volleyball Association.

His wide range of experience as a player, teacher, coach, referee, executive member, author and scholar provide Dr. Bratton with unique qualifications for preparing a text of this nature.

EXPLANATION OF SYMBOLS

Passer — starting position — face pass and set

Passer — subsequent positions — face pass and set

Passer — starting position — forearm pass and throw

Passer — subsequent positions — forearm pass and throw

Attacker — starting position — spike and tip

Attacker — subsequent positions — spike and tip

Blocker — starting position

Blocker — subsequent positions

Server

Dive or roll

Coach

Ball basket

CHAPTER ONE
PASSING DRILLS — 1 PLAYER

The first drills in this chapter are designed for beginners. They are well suited to teaching the pass to all beginners where the ideal learning situation exits of one ball for every student. Players can use the other drills for practicing and perfecting their passing skills. The player can use either a face pass or a forearm pass with most of the passing drills.

DRILL 1   **PASSING**   **1 PLAYER, 1 BALL**

The player stands 6 feet away from a wall and throws the ball against the wall about 10 to 15 feet above the floor. The player moves under the ball and catches it. He then checks his hand and body position. Concentrate on correct technique.

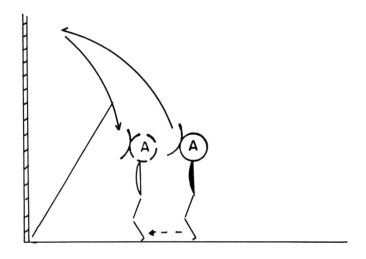

DRILL 2   **PASSING**   **1 PLAYER, 1 BALL**

The player stands close to the wall and passes the ball against the wall using a face pass. The player may use a volleyball or a basketball. The basketball will help to strengthen the forearms and fingers and will also assist in developing the proper hand position and relaxation in the wrists. Concentrate on relaxing the wrists and also on the follow through with the index fingers.

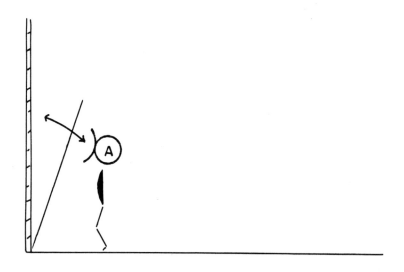

DRILL 3   **PASSING**   1 PLAYER, 1 BALL

The player stands about 5 feet away from the wall and throws the ball against the wall about 8 feet above the floor. The player moves and crouches under the ball and catches the ball. The player or coach should check the hand position to see if it is correct.

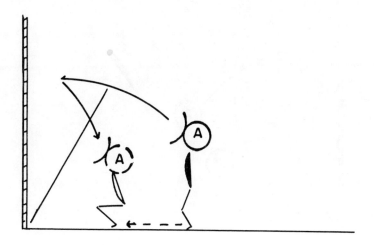

DRILL 4   **PASSING**   1 PLAYER, 1 BALL

The player stands 6 feet away from a wall and throws the ball against the wall about 10 to 15 feet above the floor. The player moves under the ball and passes it to the wall. The player then catches the next rebound and starts again. Emphasize correct technique.

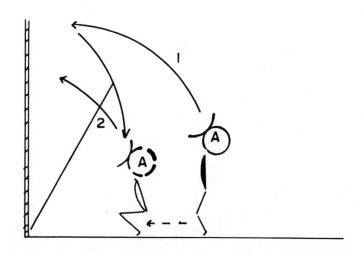

DRILL 5   **PASSING**   1 PLAYER, 1 BALL

The player stands about 8 feet away from a wall and throws a ball against the wall about 10 feet above the floor and to his right or to his left. The player moves under the ball and catches the ball using correct form. The player or coach should check the hand and body position to see if they are correct.

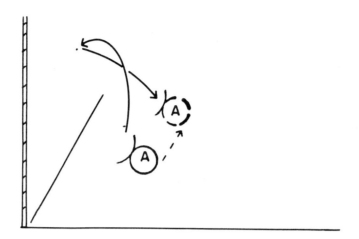

DRILL 6   **PASSING**   1 PLAYER, 1 BALL

The player stands about 5 feet away from the wall and throws the ball against the wall about 3 feet above his head. The player moves and crouches under the ball and passes the ball high against the wall. Catch the ball and repeat the drill.

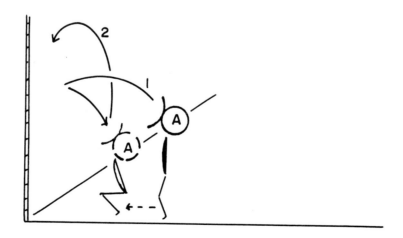

The player stands about 8 feet away from a wall and passes the ball against the wall. Concentrate on performing each pass correctly. See how many times you can pass the ball against the wall without making a mistake. Start again each time you make a mistake.

Place a line on the wall at a height of 10 feet. The player stands about 6 feet away from the wall and attempts to pass the ball to the wall above the line alternately using a face pass and a forearm pass. Repeat 30 times and rest. Start again after each error.

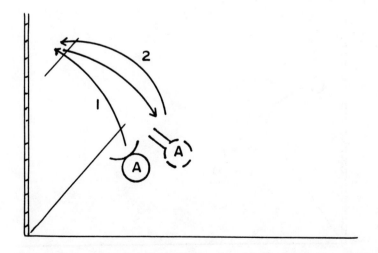

DRILL 9   **PASSING**   1 PLAYER, 1 BALL

Mark lines on the wall at heights of 8, 12 and 16 feet. The player attempts to pass the ball to the wall above the highest line. Keep score for 20 continuous passes. 16 feet — 3 points. 12 feet — 2 points, 8 feet — 1 point.

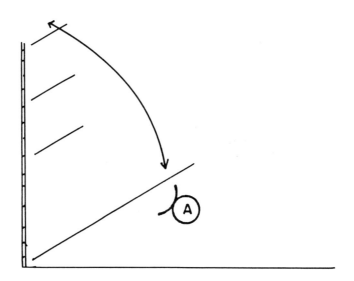

DRILL 10   **PASSING**   1 PLAYER, 1 BALL

Paint a circle on the wall about 12 feet above the floor. The circle should be slightly larger than the size of a volleyball. Have the player stand 6 feet away from the wall and pass the ball to the target 100 times. Rest after each 25 passes. Keep score on each pass that hits the target.

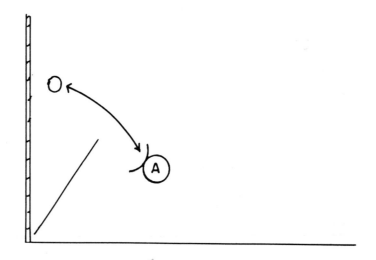

The player stands about 8 feet away from a wall and throws the ball against the wall about 10 feet above the floor and to his right or to his left. The player moves to his side and under the ball and passes the ball high against the wall. Catch the ball and repeat the drill.

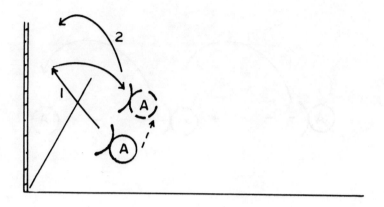

The player bounces the ball on the floor, moves under the ball and passes it high. He allows the ball to bounce on the floor and then move under the ball and pass it high again. Continue.

DRILL 13   PASSING   1 PLAYER, 1 BALL

The player passes the ball 10 feet above his head and to a spot 10 feet in front. The player runs under the ball and repeats the action. Continue. Concentrate on moving fast to get under the ball and then taking time to make the pass.

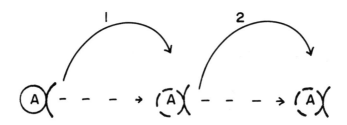

DRILL 14   PASSING   1 PLAYER, 1 BALL

The player passes 5 feet above and 10 feet in front and then runs under the ball and passes straight up using a forearm pass. He then repeats the same actions. Alternate a forearm pass with a face pass.

DRILL 15   PASSING   1 PLAYER, 1 BALL

The player passes the ball about 15 feet above his head, does a full turn, and passes the ball again.

DRILL 16   PASSING   1 PLAYER, 1 BALL

The player passes the ball about 5 feet above his head alternately using a face pass and a forearm pass. Repeat the action 15 to 30 times and rest. Start again after each error.

DRILL 17   **PASSING**   1 PLAYER, 1 BALL

The player passes the ball about 10 feet above his head, does a half turn, and passes the ball again.

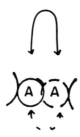

DRILL 18   **PASSING**   1 PLAYER, 1 BALL

Mark two lines on the floor 3 feet apart. The player starts outside one line with his back to the line. He passes the ball backwards over his head, turns and crosses the second line and passes the ball backwards again to the other line. Continue.

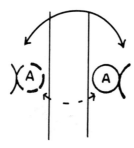

DRILL 19   **PASSING**   1 PLAYER, 1 BALL

The player passes the ball high over the net, crosses under the net, and passes the ball back over the net. Continue. Try to turn and face the net before passing the ball. Attempt to complete 15 passes.

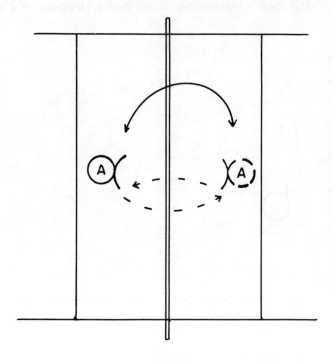

DRILL 20   **PASSING**   1 PLAYER, 1 BALL

The player passes the ball high over the net using a face pass, crosses under the net, and passes the ball over the net using a forearm pass. Continue the action using a face pass on one side of the net and a forearm pass on the other side.

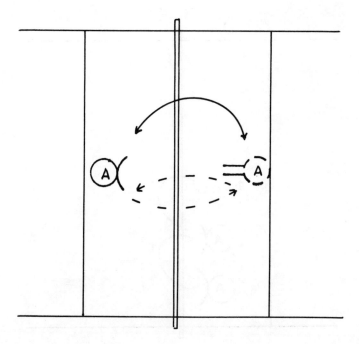

DRILL 21　　　　　　　　　　**PASSING**　　　　　　　　　1 PLAYER, 1 BALL

The player stands with his toes 1 foot away from the wall and facing the wall. Pass the ball straight up above the head so that the ball does not touch the wall and so that the player does not have to move his feet. Start again after each mistake and try to make 15 passes in a row without making a mistake.

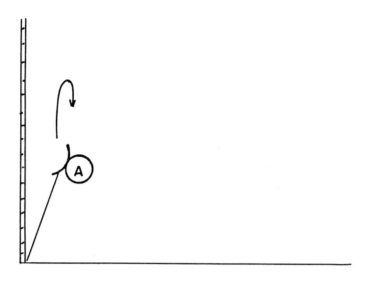

DRILL 22　　　　　　　　　　**PASSING**　　　　　　　　　1 PLAYER, 1 BALL

The player starts 3 feet away from the net and facing the net. He passes the ball about 8 feet above his head and about 3 feet to his side. He moves sideways under the ball and passes again to his side. He may always move in the same direction along the net, or he may move from side to side.

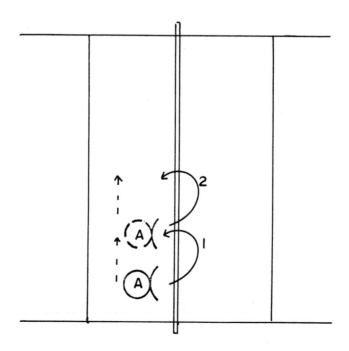

DRILL 23   **PASSING**   1 PLAYER, 1 BALL

The player stands about 6 feet away from a wall. He passes the ball against the wall and about 12 feet above the floor. He jumps as high as possible each time to make the next pass. Repeat 25 times and rest. Start again after each error.

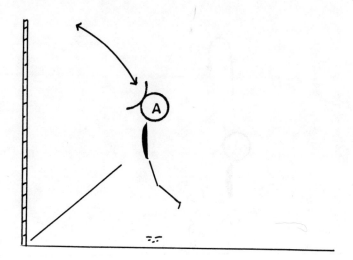

DRILL 24   **PASSING**   1 PLAYER, 1 BALL

The player passes the ball about 10 feet above his head and jumps as high as possible each time to make each pass. Repeat 15 to 25 times and rest. Start again after each error.

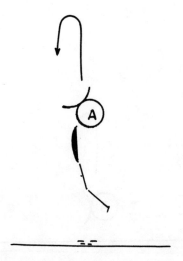

DRILL 25   **PASSING**   1 PLAYER, 1 BALL

The player passes the ball about 20 feet above his head. After each pass he sits on the floor and stands up to make the next pass. There are many variations that can be used with this drill. (push-up, squat, jump, turn, close eyes)

DRILL 26   **PASSING**   1 PLAYER, 1 BALL

The player starts 6 to 10 feet away from a wall with his back to the wall. He passes the ball straight up, turns, and runs to touch the wall and back to pass the ball again. Continue. Move farther away from the wall to make the drill more difficult.

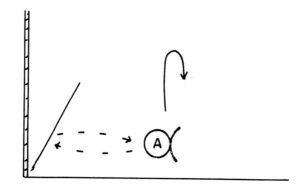

The player starts 5 feet away from the net. He throws the ball into the net at differing angles, moves under the ball and passes it high using either a face pass (with screw under) or a forearm pass.

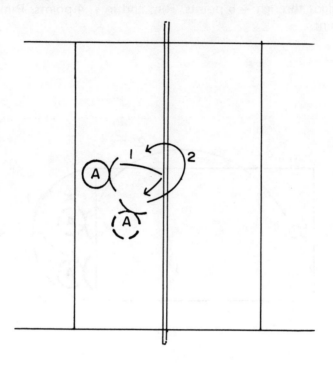

DRILL 28   **PASSING**   1 PLAYER, 1 BALL

The player stands 15 feet away from a basketball hoop. He bounces the ball on the floor, moves under the ball and attempts to pass the ball through the hoop.

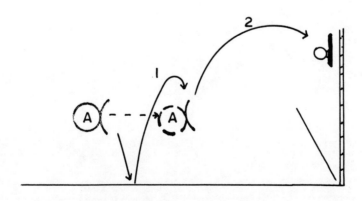

The player stands about 15 feet away from a basketball hoop. The player throws the ball above his head and to one side, moves under the ball and attempts to pass the ball through the hoop. Keep score for 20 passes. Straight through — 5 points. Rim and in — 4 points. Rim and out — 3 points. Backboard and in — 1 point.

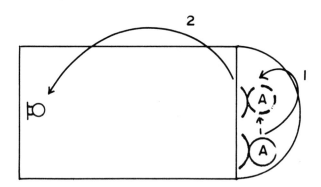

CHAPTER TWO
PASSING DRILLS — 2 PLAYERS

Drills involving two players are probably the most practical and efficient ones to use when learning a skill. The player is very active and is able to handle the ball a large number of times. Two player drills should be used extensively with beginning players. The first two drills in this chapter each explain a very effective teaching sequence for the face pass and the forearm pass. The teacher or coach must correct any faults in form early. Movement should be introduced once the proper form becomes somewhat automatic. Most of the drills involve movement.

DRILL 30   **PASSING, FACE PASS LEARNING SEQUENCE**   2 PLAYERS, 1 BALL

Player B holds his hands in front of this face in the proper passing position. Player A carefully throws the ball to B and B catches the ball. The ball should not bounce from the fingers. Repeat 20 or 30 times. Now have B move slightly and cath the ball. Repeat 20 or 30 times. Progress to having B pass the ball to A.

DRILL 31   **PASSING, FOREARM PASS LEARNING SEQUENCE**   2 PLAYERS, 1 BALL

Player B holds his arms in front of his body with the hands open and the palms up. His arms should be straight and he should be slightly crouched. Player A throws the ball to B and B catches the ball with straight arms. Repeat 20 or 30 times. Now have B move slightly to catch the ball. Repeat 20 or 30 times. Emphasize correct body and arm position. Now have B assume the appropriate hand grip for the forearm pass and have A throw to B. Player B allows the ball to bounce from the arms. Now have B progress to passing the ball back to A.

DRILL 32   **PASSING**   2 PLAYERS, 1 BALL, 2 HOOPS

Have two players start inside two hoops or circles on the floor about 10 feet apart. Attempt to make 20 consecutive passes without moving outside of the hoops.

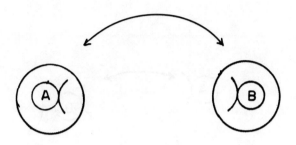

DRILL 33   **PASSING**   2 PLAYERS, 1 BALL, 4 HOOPS

Place 4 hoops or circles on the floor in a square and about 10 feet apart. Each player has two hoops and must attempt to pass the ball alternately to each of his partner's hoops so that the partner can pass while standing inside the hoop. Keep score on the number of passes each partner is able to make while standing inside his hoop. Emphasize accurate passing.

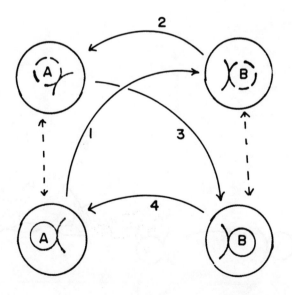

DRILL 34   **PASSING**   2 PLAYERS, 1 BALL

Two players stand about 5 feet apart and pass the ball back and forth using a flat trajectory. Emphasize the loose wrist action.

DRILL 35   **PASSING**   2 PLAYERS, 1 BALL

Two players stand about 5 feet apart and pass the ball back and forth using only the thumb and index finger of each hand to make the pass. Keep the pass flat or low. You may also use the middle finger, thus folding the ring finger and little finger into the palm. This drill will develop the desired finger action control in the face pass.

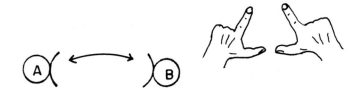

DRILL 36   **PASSING**   **2 PLAYERS, 1 BALL**

Two players start 10 feet apart. Player A throws a ball slightly to B's side forcing B to step to his side and pass the ball using a forearm pass. Player B should concentrate on playing the ball in front of the midline of his body. The throw must be accurate. Player B passes the ball accurately back to A.

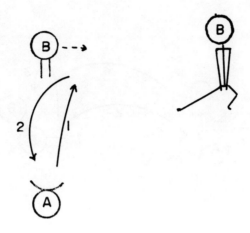

DRILL 37   **PASSING**   **2 PLAYERS, 1 BALL**

Player B starts 5 feet away from a wall and facing the wall in a low crouched position. Player A stands behind him and throws the ball to the wall in front of B. Player B must pass the ball high using either a face pass or a forearm pass.

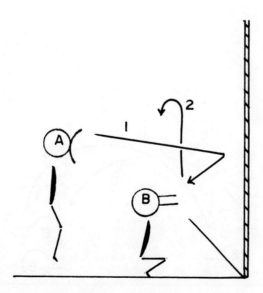

Two players stand about 15 feet apart. Player A passes the ball above his head to himself using a forearm pass and then passes the ball to B using a face pass. The drill can also be done in the reverse order.

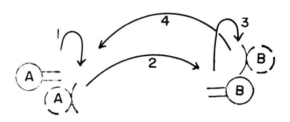

Two players stand about 15 feet apart. Player A passes the ball above his head using a forearm pass, does a half turn so that his back is to his partner, and passes the ball backwards to his partner using a forearm pass. This drill can also be done using only a face pass or a combination of face pass and forearm pass.

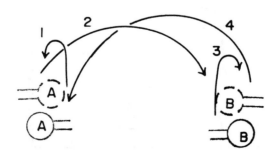

DRILL 40   PASSING   2 PLAYERS, 1 BALL

Two players start about 15 feet apart and facing each other and close to the net. Player A passes to himself using a face pass, turns 90 degrees to face the net and passes to his partner using a forearm pass.

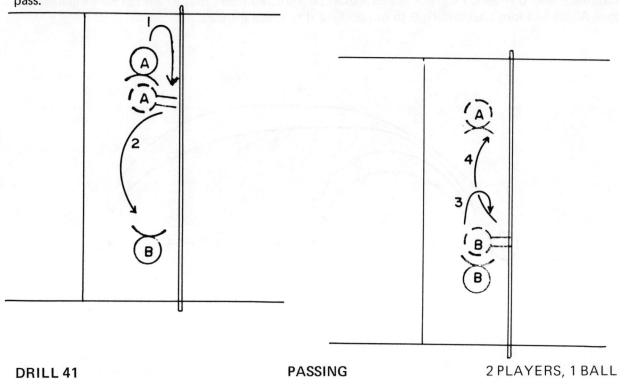

DRILL 41   PASSING   2 PLAYERS, 1 BALL

Two players start about 15 feet apart. Player A remains stationary and B moves alternately to his left and then to his right. Player B must pass the ball accurately to A. Player A passes to one side or the other forcing B to move to pass the ball. Emphasize proper body and feet alignment in this drill. Face the target.

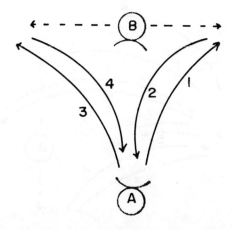

DRILL 42   PASSING   2 PLAYERS, 1 BALL

Two players start 20 feet apart. One player remains stationary and the other moves forward and backward to make the pass. The ball must be passed accurately to the stationary player. Player A is stationary and B moves. Player A makes a short pass forcing B to run forward to make the pass and then A makes a long pass forcing B to run backward to make the pass.

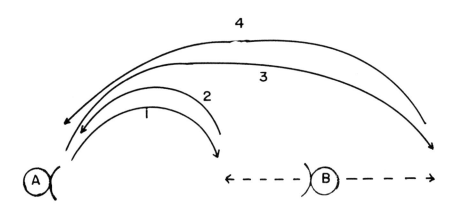

DRILL 43   PASSING   2 PLAYERS, 1 BALL

Player A remains stationary and B moves. Start about 15 feet apart. Player A passes the ball to B's right, then to his left, then in front, and then behind. Keep the passes low so that B must move rapidly.

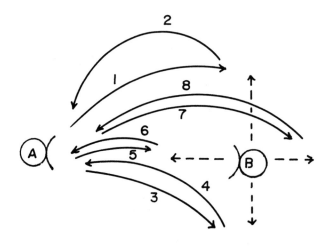

DRILL 44   **PASSING**   **2 PLAYERS, 1 BALL**

Two players stand about 15 feet apart. Player A is erect and B is in a low crouched position. Player A passes the ball low and flat to B and B passes the ball high and directly to A. Change after 25 passes. Try to use the face pass only.

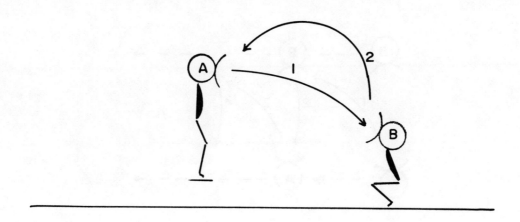

DRILL 45   **PASSING**   **2 PLAYERS, 1 BALL**

Player B sits on the floor, Player A throws a ball to B forcing B to roll backward while passing the ball high and back to A.

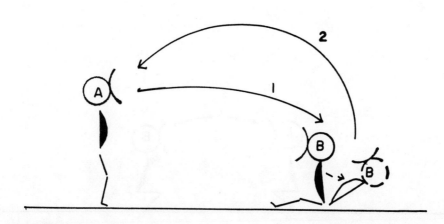

DRILL 46 PASSING 2 PLAYERS, 1 BALL

Two players start 10 feet apart and facing each other. They move laterally down the floor passing the ball ahead to the partner. Keep the passes fairly low.

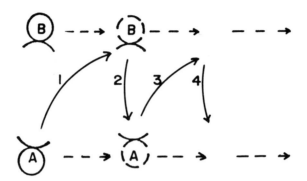

DRILL 47 PASSING 2 PLAYERS, 1 BALL

Two players stand about 8 feet apart in a low crouched position and pass the ball back and forth. Keep the pass low and fast and try not to stand up to make the pass. Rest after 20 passes.

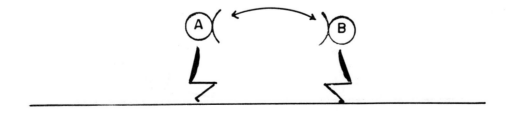

Two players start facing each other in a deep crouched position and about 10 feet apart. They hop laterally down the floor and stay in the deep crouched pposition while passing.

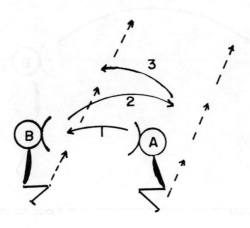

Two players start about 5 feet apart. The players jump each time they make a pass. The pass should be low so that the players have to jump rapidly.

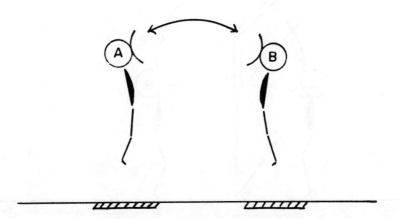

DRILL 50   **PASSING**   **2 PLAYERS, 1 BALL**

Two players start about 15 feet apart. The players jump each time they make the pass and pass at the height of their jump. Keep the passes high and accurate.

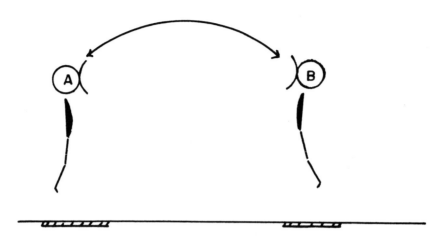

DRILL 51   **PASSING**   **2 PLAYERS, 1 BALL**

Two players stand about 5 feet back from the net and pass the ball back and forth over the net. Set a goal of 20 passes in a row without a mistake. Start again after each mistake.

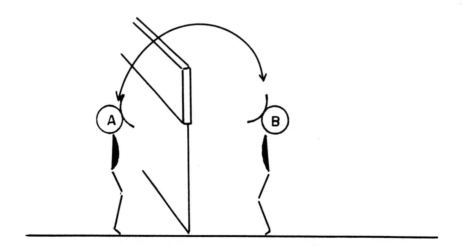

DRILL 52   **PASSING**   2 PLAYERS, 1 BALL

Two players start about 5 feet back from the net and pass the ball back and forth over the net using a jump pass. Keep the passes low forcing rapid movement. Catch the ball and start again when the pass is out of control.

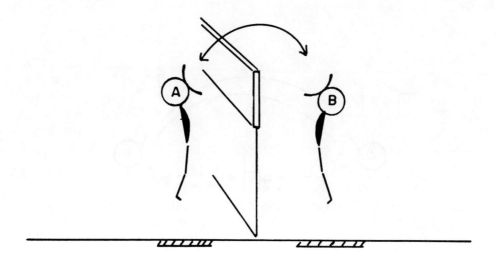

DRILL 53   **PASSING**   2 PLAYERS, 1 BALL

Two players start on opposite sides of the net and about 5 feet away from the net. They pass the ball back and forth alternately to the left and to the right thus forcing the partner to move to his side to pass the ball. Keep the passes low so that they must move rapidly.

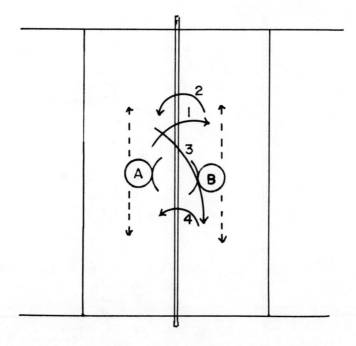

DRILL 54   PASSING   2 PLAYERS, 1 BALL, 1 CHAIR

Two players start 20 feet apart and facing each other with the chair halfway between them. Player A passes to B and then runs to touch the chair and back to his position. Player B passes the ball to himself and then to A and runs and touches the chair and back to his position.

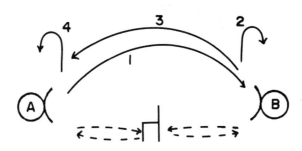

DRILL 55   PASSING   2 PLAYERS, 1 BALL

Each player starts 10 feet in from each sideline and facing each other. Player A passes high to B and then runs back to touch his sideline. Player B passes high to A and then runs back to touch his sideline.

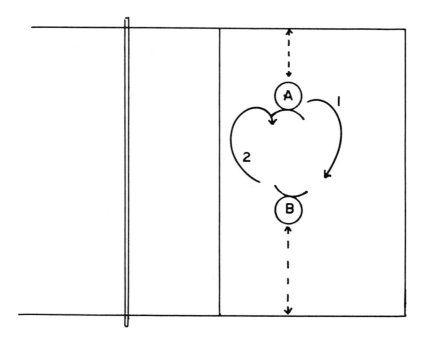

DRILL 56   PASSING   2 PLAYERS, 1 BALL, 2 CHAIRS

Two players start beside the net and 25 feet apart. The two chairs are placed on the attack line and even with the two players. Player A passes to B and then runs around the chair and back to the net. Player B passes to himself and then passes to A and runs around the chair. This drill can be done with four players and the players must pass directly back to the other side.

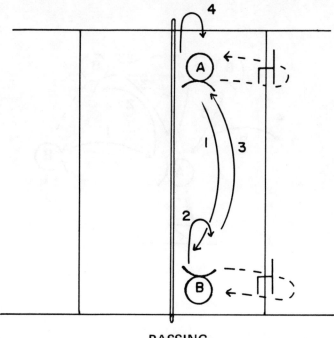

DRILL 57   PASSING   2 PLAYERS, 1 BALL

Two players start about 15 feet apart. Player A remains stationary and B moves in a circle around A. Try to keep the distance the same and B must pass the ball accurately back to A. Player A must pass the ball far enough in front of the moving player B to force him to move rapidly to make the pass. Emphasize proper body and feet alignment and attempt to hurry and be stationary when the pass is made.

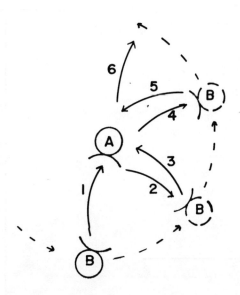

DRILL 58   **PASSING**   2 PLAYERS, 1 BALL

Two players start about 15 feet apart. Player A remains stationary and B moves in a circle around A. Player B passes the ball low and flat to A forcing him to crouch each time he passes the ball. Player A must pass the ball high and ahead of B. Emphasize facing the target.

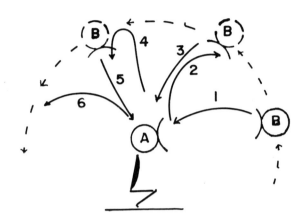

DRILL 59   **PASSING**   2 PLAYERS, 1 BALL

Two players start 5 feet apart and facing each other and close to the net or a wall. Each time they pass the ball they take one step backward until they are 30 feet apart. They then take one step forward each time they pass the ball.

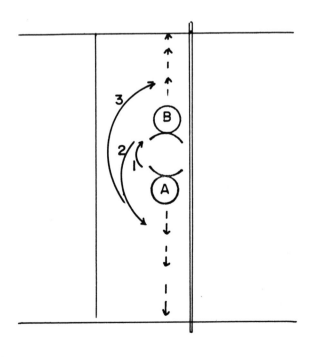
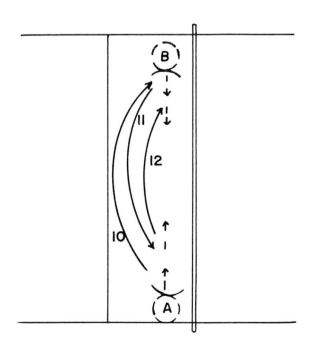

DRILL 60   **PASSING**   **2 PLAYERS, 1 BALL**

Two players start 5 feet apart and facing each other and close to the net or a wall. They must jump high each time they pass. Each time they pass they take one step backward until they are 30 feet apart. They then take one step forward each time they pass the ball. Keep the passes high and accurate. This is a good drill to have the players go back and start again every time they make a mistake.

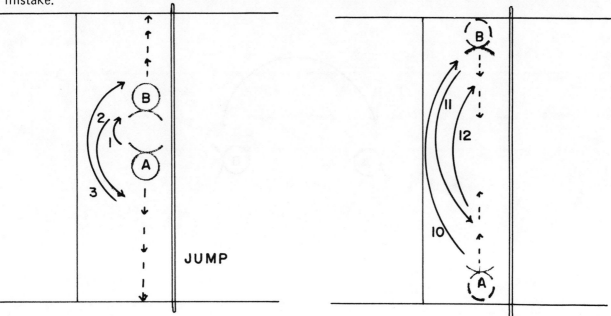

DRILL 61   **PASSING**   **2 PLAYERS, 1 BALL**

Two players start about 15 feet apart. The players turn 90 degrees in the same direction after each pass. The first pass is forward, the second is sideways, the third is backward, the fourth is sideways, and the fifth is forward. Practice this drill beside a net or wall to encourage accuracy.

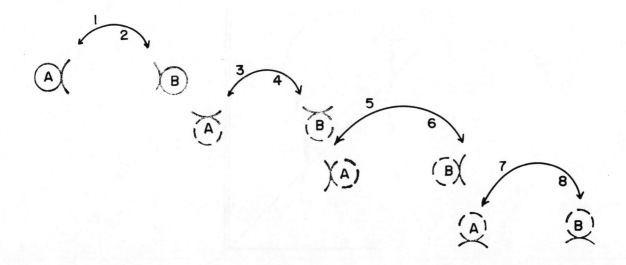

Two players stand about 10 feet apart with their backs to each other and pass the ball backwards to each other. Keep the passes high.

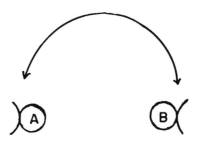

Two players start facing a wall about 15 feet apart and close to the wall. The players pass the ball sideways without touching the wall. Advanced players should try this drill using a jump pass sideways.

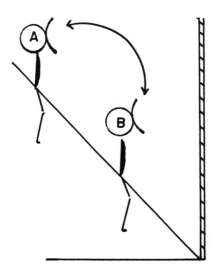

DRILL 64   **PASSING**   **2 PLAYERS, 1 BALL**

Two players start in diagonally opposite corners of the court and pass back and forth. The player in the back corner should try to make a high accurate set to the net.

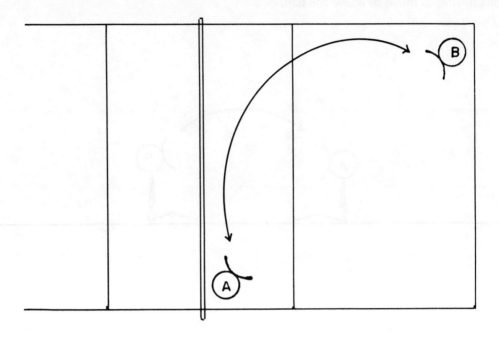

DRILL 65   **PASSING**   **2 PLAYERS, 1 BALL**

Player A remains stationary at the net and close to the sideline. Player B starts in the opposite back corner. Each time B passes the ball he takes one step forward until he is only 5 feet away from A. He then takes one step backward each time he passes the ball until he is in the corner. Player B must concentrate on making a perfect set each time.

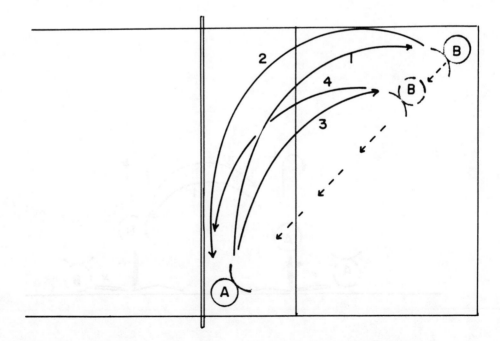

41

DRILL 66　　　　　　　　　　**PASSING**　　　　　　　　**2 PLAYERS, 1 BALL**

Two players sit on the floor facing each other and about 10 feet apart. They pass the ball back and forth. Have a contest in the class or team to see which partners can make 20 consecutive passes without having to move to chase the ball.

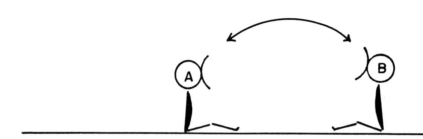

DRILL 67　　　　　　　　　　**PASSING**　　　　　　　　**2 PLAYERS, 1 BALL**

Two players sit facing each other and about 10 feet apart. Player A passes to player B and then does one sit-up. Player B passes the ball to himself and then passes to player A and B now does one sit-up.

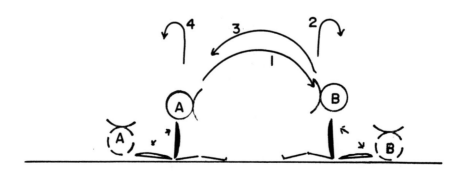

DRILL 68   PASSING   2 PLAYERS, 1 BALL

Two players lie on their front on the floor about 8 feet apart. They pass the ball back and forth by arching and flipping the ball with the fingers. Keep the pass low.

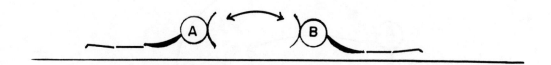

DRILL 69   PASSING   2 PLAYERS, 1 BALL

Two players lie on their back on the floor about 5 feet apart. They pass the ball back and forth from this position using the fingers.

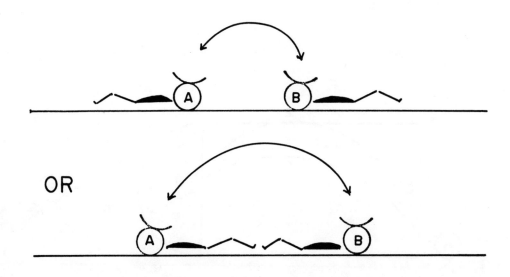

DRILL 70   PASSING   2 PLAYERS, 1 BALL

Player A is standing and B starts about 10 feet away and in a low crouched position. Player A throws a ball to B forcing B to fall backwards while passing the ball. Player B rolls and recovers. Player A then throws the ball at B again. Player B should try to make a high pass to A.

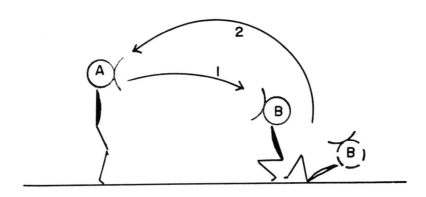

DRILL 71   PASSING   2 PLAYERS, 1 BALL

Player A stands under the basketball hoop and the other player starts outside the head of the key. Player A throws or sets the ball to the free throw line and player B moves under the ball and attempts to pass the ball through the hoop.

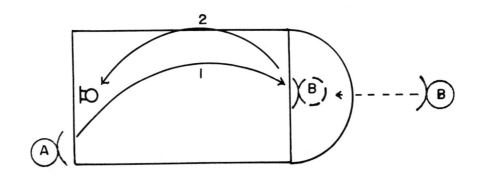

44

DRILL 72   PASSING   2 PLAYERS, 1 BALL

Player A stands to the side of the key and player B starts under the basketball hoop. Player A throws or sets the ball to the free throw line and B moves under the ball and passes backwards through the hoop. The pass could also be forward thus forcing B to turn and face the target.

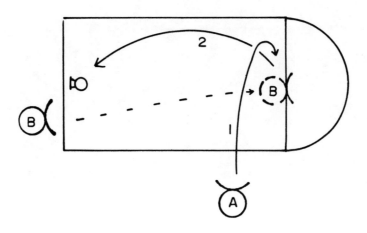

DRILL 73   PASSING, HEEL OF THE HAND   2 PLAYERS, 1 BALL

Two players pass the ball back and forth using the heel of the hand or base of the hand to pass the ball. Practice using the left hand as well as the right hand. This drill can be done close to the net.

CHAPTER THREE
PASSING DRILLS — 3 PLAYERS

Three player drills permit the player to practice the skill as it would be performed in a game. The ball comes in at one angle and goes out at a different angle. Setting techniques and the backward pass can be learned and developed. Many of the drills in this chapter are designed for learning and practicing setting skills. The face pass or the forearm pass can be utilized in most of the drills.

DRILL 74 PASSING 3 PLAYERS, 1 BALL

Three players start about 15 feet apart and in a triangle. Player A starts and the ball is passed around the triangle. Concentrate on footwork and body alignment. Face the target.

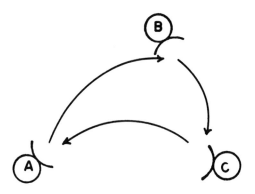

DRILL 75 PASSING 3 PLAYERS, 1 BALL

Three players start 15 feet apart and in a triangle. The ball is passed from A to B to C to A around the triangle. Player A passes low to B and B passes high to C. Player C passes low to A and A passes high to B. Continue. Concentrate on turning the body to face the target.

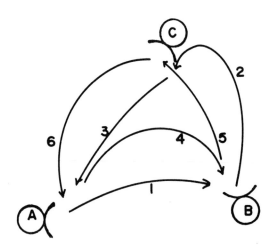

DRILL 76   **PASSING**   **3 PLAYERS, 1 BALL**

Player A hits or tips to player B, and B passes to C using a forearm pass. Player C passes to himself and hits or tips to player A. Player A passes to B using a forearm pass. Continue. Concentrate on body position and feet alignment.

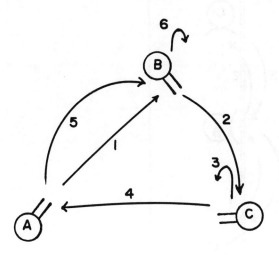

DRILL 77   **PASSING**   **3 PLAYERS, 1 BALL**

Three players start 10 feet apart and in a triangle. The first time a player receives a pass he passes back to the passer. The next time he passes to the other player. The ball goes from A to B to A to B to C to B to C to A. Keep the passes low and fast.

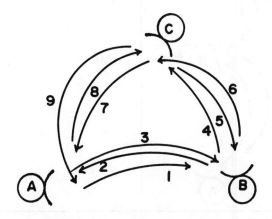

DRILL 78   **PASSING**   3 PLAYERS, 1 BALL

Three players start 10 feet apart and close to the net. The two outside players face the middle player and pass forward to him and close to the net. The middle player must set sideways to the third player.

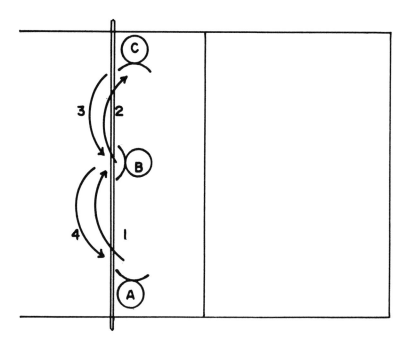

DRILL 79   **PASSING**   3 PLAYERS, 1 BALL

Three players start 10 feet apart and close to the net. The two outside players face the middle player and pass forward to him and close to the net. The middle player takes one step towards the net, jumps to fake an attack, and sets sideways to the third player. He then lands and steps back quickly for the next pass.

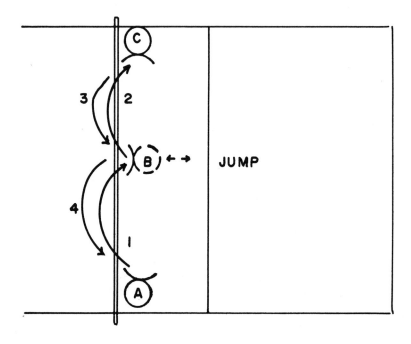

DRILL 80   **PASSING**   3 PLAYERS, 1 BALL

Player A starts at the sideline and close to the net. Player B starts on the attack line in the middle, and C starts on the attack line and at the sideline. The ball is passed from A to B to C to A and close to the net. Each player moves back and forth between the net and the attack line after each pass.

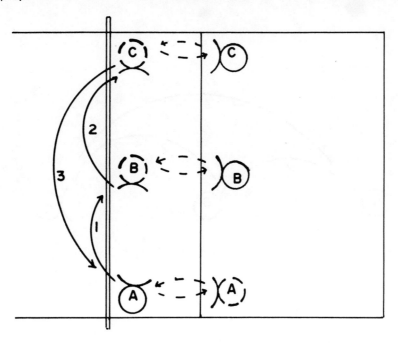

DRILL 81.   **PASSING**   3 PLAYERS, 1 BALL

Three players start 15 feet apart and on the attack line. Player A throws the ball up close to the middle of the net and B must move and turn under the ball and set forward to C. Player C then passes back to B and B must again turn under the ball and set forward to A. Players A and C move back to the attack line after they pass. Concentrate on turning completely to face the target.

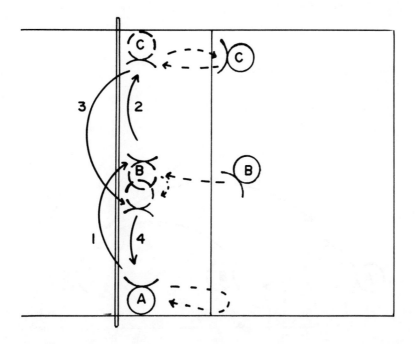

DRILL 82   **PASSING**   3 PLAYERS, 1 BALL

Three players start about 15 feet apart and in a line. Player A passes forward to B and B passes backward to C. Player C passes forward to A. Do this drill beside a net to encourage accuracy.

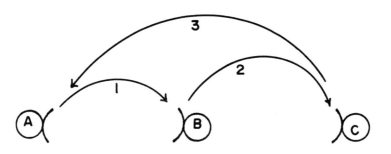

DRILL 83   **PASSING**   3 PLAYERS, 1 BALL

Three players start in a line about 10 feet apart. Player A passes forward to B and B passes backward to C. Players A and B then change places. Player C then passes forward to B. Keep moving.

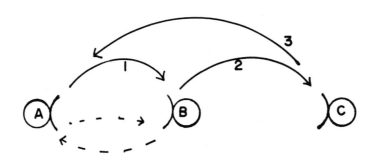

DRILL 84   PASSING   3 PLAYERS, 1 BALL

Three players stand in a line and 15 feet apart. Player B is in the middle and always passes backwards, Players A and C always pass forward to B. The ball is passed from A to B to C to B to A. Player B must turn 180 degrees after he passes to be ready for the next pass. Change positions regularly. Do the drill beside a net to help develop a backward set.

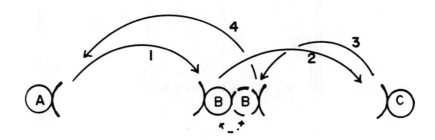

DRILL 85   PASSING   3 PLAYERS, 1 BALL

Three players start 15 feet apart and in a line. The middle player must jump each time he passes. The ball is passed from A to B to A to C to B to C to A.

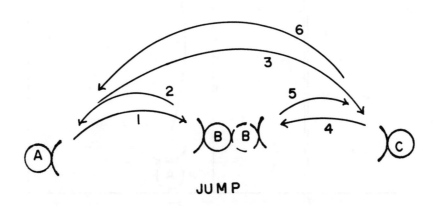

JUMP

53

DRILL 86   **PASSING**   3 PLAYERS, 1 BALL

Player A starts at the net and passes the ball straight up. Players B and C start at the attack line and B moves under the ball and passes straight up. Player C then moves under the ball and passes straight up. It may be necessary to place a chair on the attack line to force the players to move around the chair after they pass.

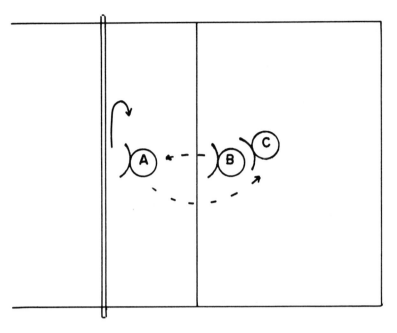

DRILL 87   **PASSING**   3 PLAYERS, 1 BALL

Players A and C start on one side of the court and B starts on the other side. Player A passes to B and moves to take B's place. Player B passes to C and moves to take C's place. Continue.

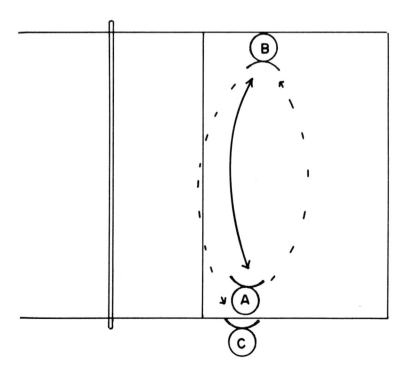

DRILL 88   PASSING   3 PLAYERS, 1 BALL

Two players start about 10 feet in from one side-line and one player starts about 10 feet in from the other side-line. Player A passes to B using a jump pass and then moves to take B's place. Player B passes to C using a jump pass and then moves to take C's place. Continue. Do this drill beside a net or wall to encourage accurate setting.

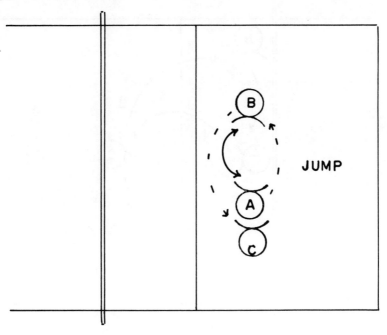

DRILL 89   PASSING   3 PLAYERS, 1 BALL

Three players start 15 feet apart and close to the net. Player A throws the ball to a point 10 feet back from the net and 10 feet in from the side-line. Player C must run the ball and pass it to B and return to his starting position. Player B passes to A and continue.

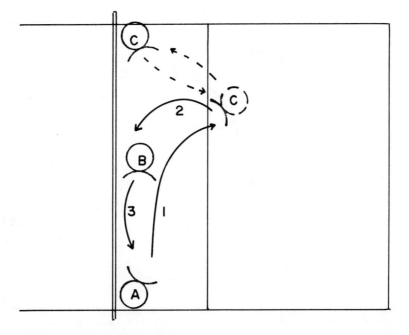

Players A and B start at the net and 15 feet apart. Player C starts at the aide-line and 15 feet back from the net. Player A passes the ball to the centre of the court and C must move sideways, pass the ball to B and run back to the side-line. Player B passes to A and continue. Concentrate on being stationary before making the pass.

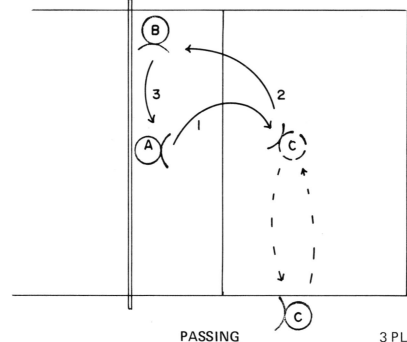

Players A and B start 15 feet apart and close to the net. Player C starts on the back line. Player A passes to a point about 15 feet back from the net. Player C must run forward, pass the ball to B, and run back to the back line. Player B passes to A. Continue. It may be necessary for A to pass to himself if C is not fast enough.

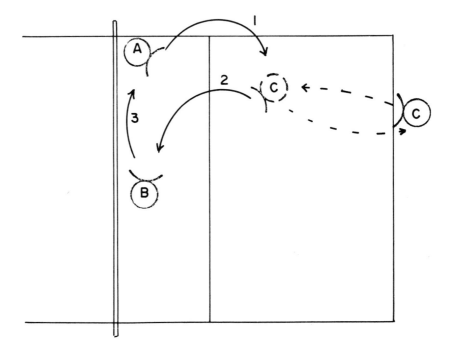

Two players start in the front corners of the court and one player starts in one of the back corners. The ball is passed from A to B to C. Players A and B must concentrate on making perfect sets.

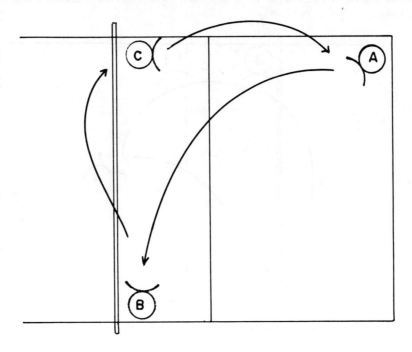

Player A starts on the back line and midway between the side-lines. Players B and C start at the net and on the side-lines. Player A passes alternately to B and C to start each sequence. Player B passes to C and C passes somehwere in court forcing A to move forward to make the next pass. If the ball is in the left side of the court, the ball should be passed to the right. If the ball is in the right side of the court, the ball should be passed to the left. Player A should try to make a perfect set on this pass and then return to the back line to start the sequence again.

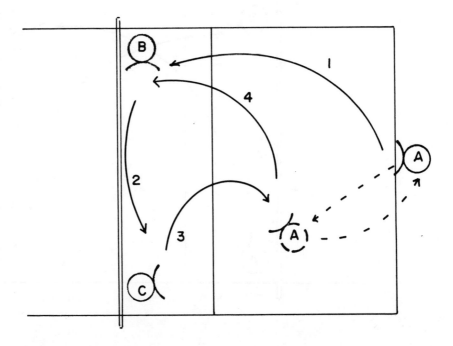

DRILL 94   PASSING   3 PLAYERS, 1 BALL

Player A starts in the centre of the court. Players B and C start on the attack line and close to the side-lines. Player A passes to the net in front of B and B moves under the pass and passes across court and close to the net to C. Player C passes back to A. Players B and C must return to the attack line after they pass.

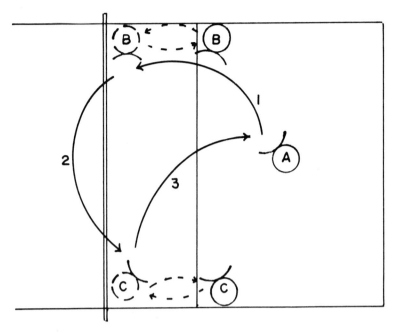

DRILL 95   PASSING   3 PLAYERS, 2 BALLS

Players A and B start at the side-lines and close to the net. Player C starts on the back line. Player A passes to the back right corner and C moves under the ball and sets the ball back to A. Player B then passes his ball to the back left corner and C moves under the ball and sets the ball back to B. Continue. It may be necessary for A and B to pass the ball to themselves twice before passing to C again.

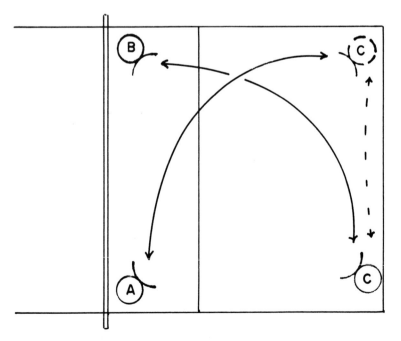

DRILL 96   PASSING   3 PLAYERS, 1 BALL

Player A stands on a table on one side of the net. Players B and C start on the other side of the net and 15 feet back from the net. Player A throws or hits a ball at B. Player B passes to C and C sets to player A who reaches over the net to provide a target with his hands.

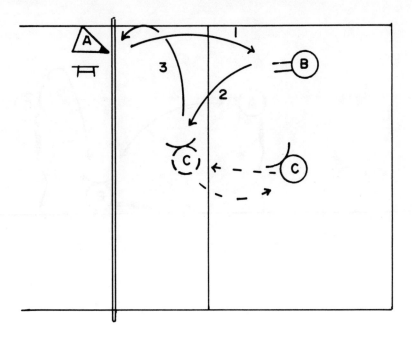

DRILL 97   PASSING   3 PLAYERS, 15 BALLS, BLANKET

Hang a blanket over the net. Player A starts about 15 feet back from the net. Player B starts on the other side of the net and behind the blanket. Player B throws the balls over the net and A must move under the ball and set it to a target. The third player collects balls.

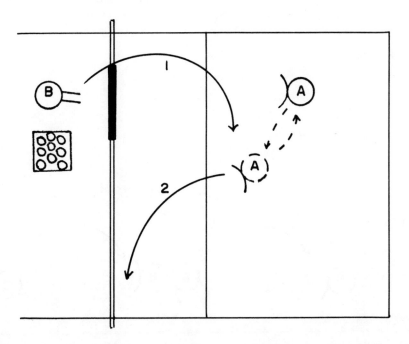

Player B starts on his back on the floor. Player A stands at his feet and C stands at his head. Both A and C have a ball and alternate passing the balls to B.

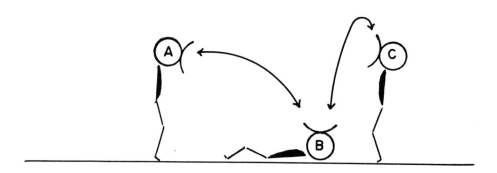

Three players start 15 feet apart and in a line. Players A and C start with the balls. The middle player must turn 180 degrees to make each pass and must turn rapidly to keep each ball going. Players A and B pass one ball and B and C pass the other ball.

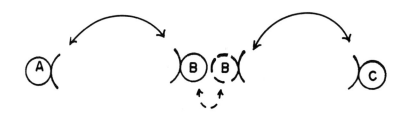

DRILL 100   **PASSING**   **3 PLAYERS, 2 BALLS**

Three players start about 15 feet apart and in a triangle. Players A and B start with the balls. The balls are passed around the triangle from A to B to C.

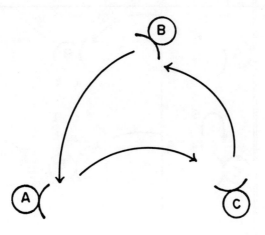

DRILL 101   **PASSING**   **3 PLAYERS, 2 BALLS**

Players B and C stand beside each other and A starts about 10 feet in front of them. Players A and C start with a ball. Player A passes to B while C passes to A. Keep the two balls moving alternately.

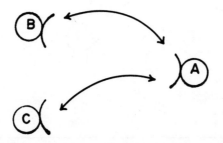

DRILL 102   **PASSING**   3 PLAYERS, 2 BALLS

Players A and C start about 15 feet apart and close to the net. Both A and C start with a ball. Player B starts opposite A and 15 feet away. Player B must move from side to side to pass the balls back to A and C. Players A and C pass the ball once to themselves and then pass the ball straight forward to B.

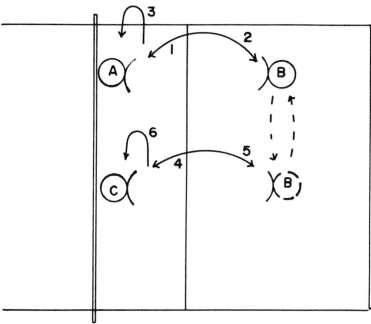

DRILL 103   **PASSING**   3 PLAYERS, 15 BALLS

Player A starts at the back line. Player B starts close to the net with his back to A. Player A throws a ball high into the court and yells "now". Player B must turn, move to the ball, and set it to C. Continue rapidly.

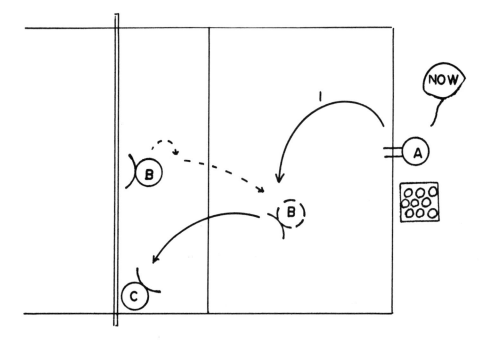

DRILL 104   PASSING   3 PLAYERS, 15 BALLS

Player A starts at the net. Players B and C start in the centre of the court. Player A throws each ball high somewhere in the court and B and C alternate setting to a target. Keep moving rapidly.

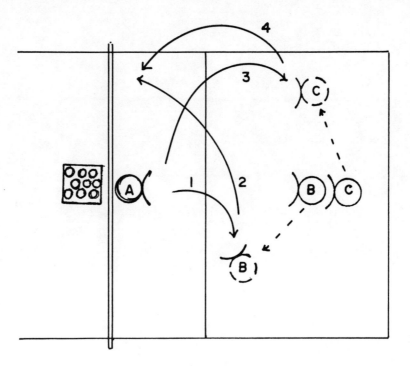

CHAPTER FOUR
PASSING DRILLS — 4 or MORE PLAYERS

The majority of the drills in this chapter are motivational or high interest drills. They can be used to add variety to lessons and practices. They require a fair degree of skill and are generally not suited for beginners. They should be used by the coach to help develop team spirit. By setting goals of 25 or 50 consecutive passes, the coach can provide the students or players with a specific challenge.

DRILL 105   **PASSING**   **4 PLAYERS, 1 BALL**

Two players start on each side of the net. The ball is passed back and forth over the net. The players move to the back of their own line after they pass.

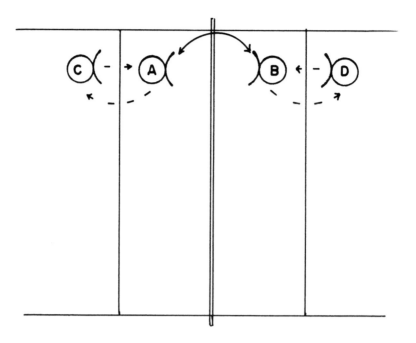

DRILL 106   **PASSING**   **4 PLAYERS, 1 BALL**

Two players start on each side of the court and close to the net. The ball is passed back and forth across court. The players move to the back of their own line after they pass.

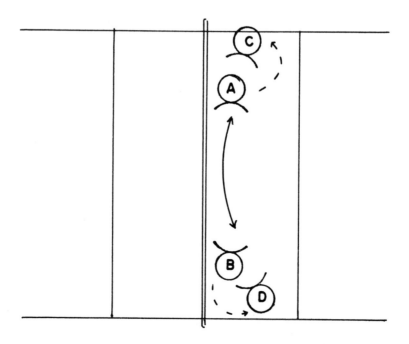

DRILL 107   **PASSING**   **4 PLAYERS, 1 BALL**

Two players start on each side of the court and close to the net. The ball is passed back and forth close to the net. The player moves across court after making his pass. This is a good drill to use as a team warm up. Establish a goal of 20 or 30 consecutive passes. Start at 0 after each error.

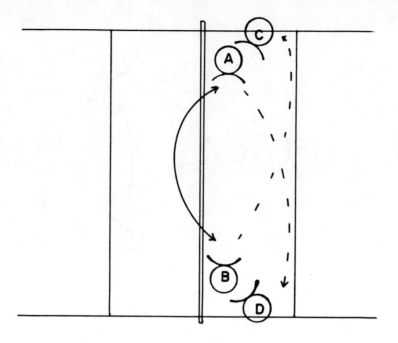

DRILL 108   **PASSING**   **4 PLAYERS, 1 BALL**

Two players start about 10 feet in from each side-line and close to the net. The players make a jump set and move to the back of the other line. Follow the pass. This is a good team warm up drill if it is used in combination with drill #107. Establish a goal of 20 or 30 consecutive passes. Start at 0 after each error.

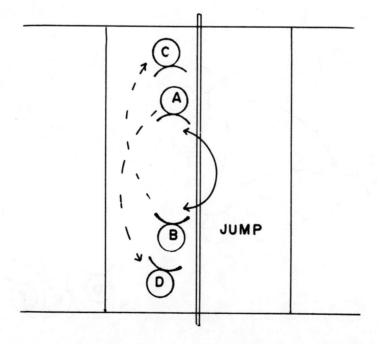

DRILL 109   PASSING   4 PLAYERS, 1 BALL

Three players start about 15 feet apart and in a triangle. Player D starts in the same corner as A. The ball is passed around the triangle and the players move to take the position of the player to whom they passed the ball.

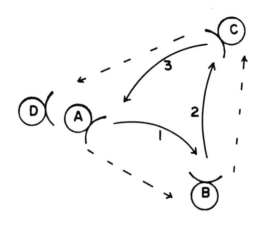

DRILL 110   PASSING   6 PLAYERS, 1 BALL

Three players start in a triangle about 15 feet apart. Three players start in a line about 10 feet away from player A. As A passes the ball, the first player in line moves to take A's position. Player A moves to take B's position and B moves to take C's position and C moves to the end of the line.

DRILL 111   PASSING   6 PLAYERS, 1 BALL

Two players start in each corner of a triangle about 20 feet apart. Each pass goes to a point midway between the players and also in the form of a triangle. The player must move from his line and under the ball to make the pass. The player follows his pass to take the position of the receiver.

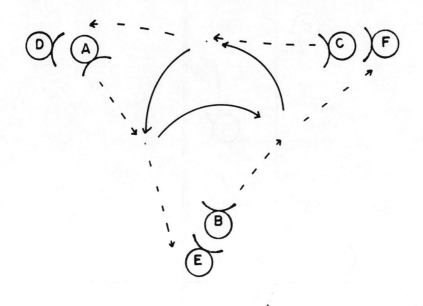

DRILL 112   PASSING   4 PLAYERS, 1 BALL

Two players start at each side-line and about 10 feet back from the net. The ball is set across court and close to the net. The players must wait until the set has been made before moving up to the net and setting the ball. After setting the player moves back to the attack line.

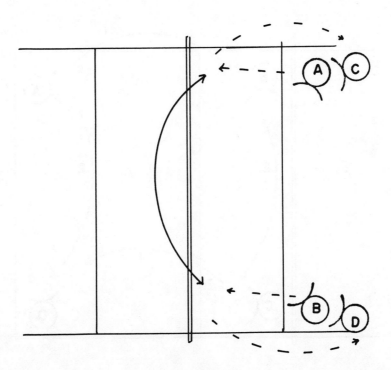

DRILL 113   PASSING   4 PLAYERS, 1 BALL

Player A starts close to the net and passes the ball straight up. Player B then moves under the ball and passes it straight up. Player C is next and then D. Move to the other side of the court after passing the ball. Try to keep the ball in the same place.

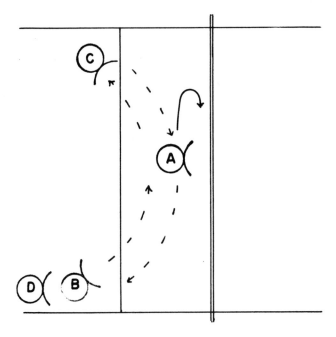

DRILL 114   PASSING   4 PLAYERS, 2 BALLS

Each player starts in one corner of the court. Players A and C start with the two balls. Pass the balls from corner to corner and try to keep the height of the passes uniform.

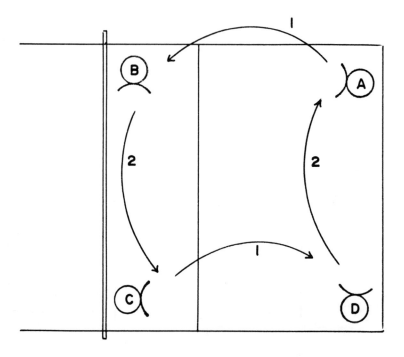

DRILL 115   PASSING   4 PLAYERS, 2 BALLS

Each player stands in one corner of the court. Players A and C pass one ball back and forth and players B and D pass the other ball.

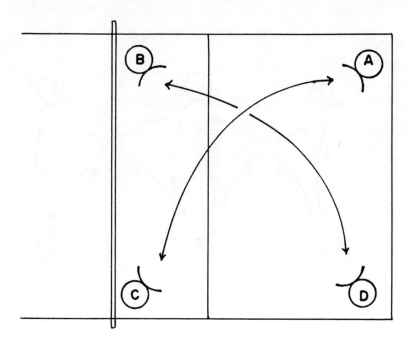

DRILL 116   PASSING   6 PLAYERS, 1 BALL

The players start in a circle about 5 feet apart. The ball is passed in a triangle from positions A to C to E. The players move in a circle around the points of the triangle. This drill can be performed with a larger circle and harder running. Concentrate on facing the target.

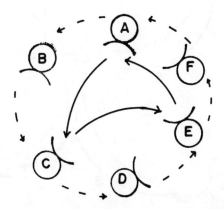

DRILL 117   **PASSING**   6 PLAYERS, 2 BALLS

Three players start in two rows about 15 feet apart. One ball is passed from A to B to C to D to A.
The other ball is passed from C to D to E to F to C. Change positions after 50 consecutive passes.
This is a good drill to have a competition between the two sides.

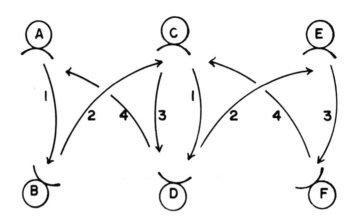

DRILL 118   **PASSING**   5 PLAYERS, 1 BALL

Four players start in a square about 20 feet apart. The fifth player starts in the centre. The centre
player alternates front passes and back passes to the outside players. With advanced players the
centre player can also perform side passes.

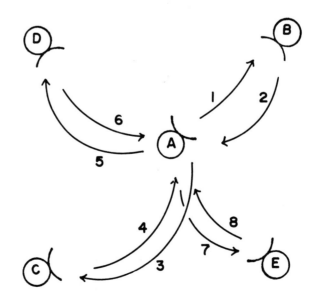

72

DRILL 119 **PASSING** 6 PLAYERS, 3 BALLS

Three players start 15 feet apart and close to the net. Three other players start in a line on one side of the court and 10 feet away from the net. These three players move sideways across the court and pass the balls with each of the front or net players. The net players may have to pass to themselves while waiting. One or two more players can be added to the moving line.

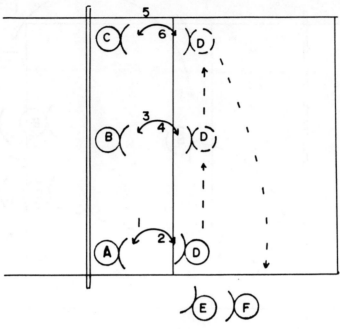

DRILL 120 **PASSING** 3 OR MORE PLAYERS, 5 BALLS

Player A starts on his back on the back line with the other two players standing behind him. Player A must do two sit-ups, stand, and run to the net. As A stands, B throws a ball high and towards the net. Player A must run under the ball and pass it to a target. Repeat the sequence with B running and C throwing. Player A collects his ball and returns to the line.

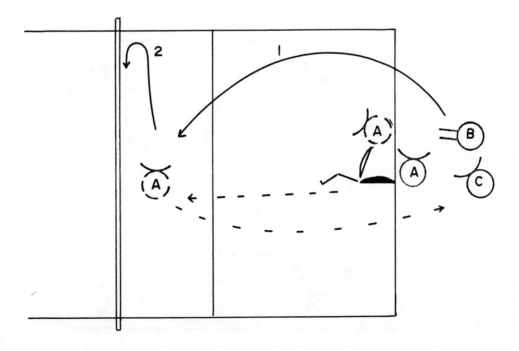

DRILL 121   PASSING   5 OR MORE PLAYERS, 10 BALLS

Player A stands at one back corner and throws balls high into the court. Players B and C start on the back line and one runs to pass the ball and the other runs to a position to hit the pass. The pass may be hit or caught. The players should learn to talk to each other on this drill. Players D and E now replace B and C and B and C rush back to the line.

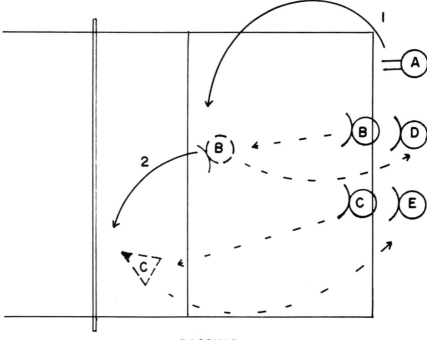

DRILL 122   PASSING   5 PLAYERS, 1 BALL

One player starts in each corner of the court. The fifth player starts in the same corner as player A. Pass the ball around the square and follow the pass to take the place of the intended receiver. Keep the passes high and accurate.

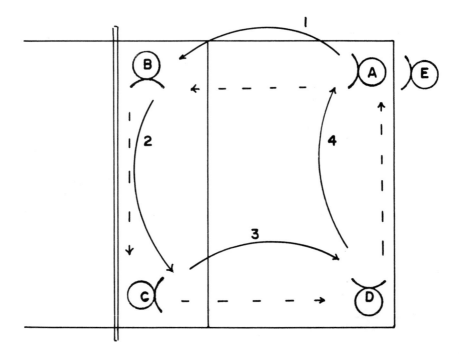

74

DRILL 123   **PASSING**   **8 PLAYERS, 3 BALLS**

Two players start in each corner of the court. Players A, B, and C start with the balls. The three balls are passed simultaneously from one corner to the next. The player follows his pass to the next corner to take the position of the receiver.

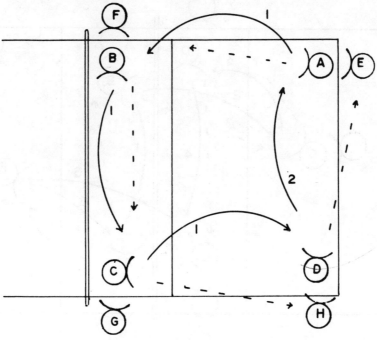

DRILL 124   **PASSING**   **8 PLAYERS, 2 BALLS**

Two players start in each corner of the court. The two balls are passed diagonally back and forth between the two corners. The players move to the next corner around the court after they pass the ball.

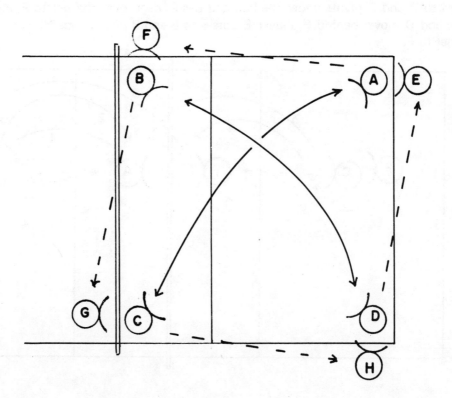

DRILL 125   **PASSING**   **12 PLAYERS, 1 BALL**

Six players start on each side of the net as indicated. The ball is passed from the positions occupied by and in order from A to B to C to D to E to F. The player follows his pass and takes the position of the person he passed to. This is a good drill to set a goal of 25 continuous passes. Start again after each mistake.

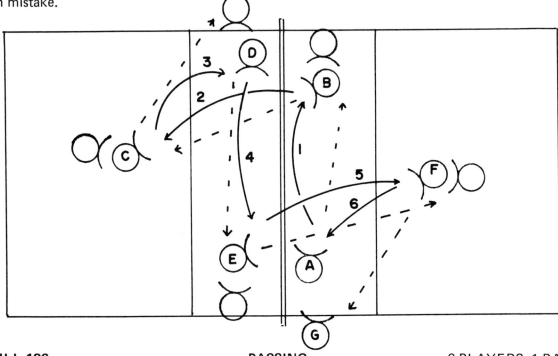

DRILL 126   **PASSING**   **6 PLAYERS, 1 BALL**

Three players start in a line on each side of the net with one player close to the net and the other two 15 feet back from the net. Player A passes to B and B passes to A. Player A pivots under the ball and passes deep over the net to C. Player B now takes A's place and B moves behind E. Player C passes to D and D pivots under the ball and passes deep over the net to E. Player C now takes D's place and D moves behind F. Player E passes to B and B pivots under the ball and passes deep over the net to F.

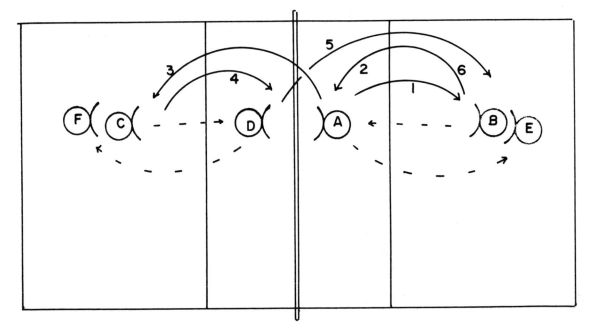

Three players start on each side of the net. One players is close to the net and the other two are 15 feet back from the net. Player A passes forward to B and B passes forward to A. Player A pivots under the ball and passes forward over the net to C. Player B now takes A's place and A moves behind E. Player C passes backward to D and D passes forward to C. Player C pivots under the ball and passes forward over the net to E. Player D now takes C's place and C moves behind F. Be sure that the net player pivots completely under the ball and faces his target.

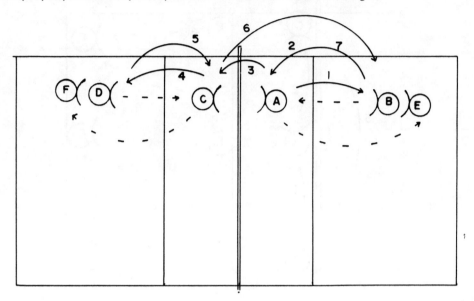

DRILL 128   **PASSING, COVERING**   5–7 PLAYERS, 1 BALL

Players A and B start close to the net and near each side line. Three players start in a line in the centre of the court. Player C passes to A and moves to cover. Player A passes low back to C and C passes back to A. Player A now passes across court to B and C moves to cover B. Player B now passes low to C and C passes back to B. Player B passes to D and the sequence is repeated with D taking C's place.

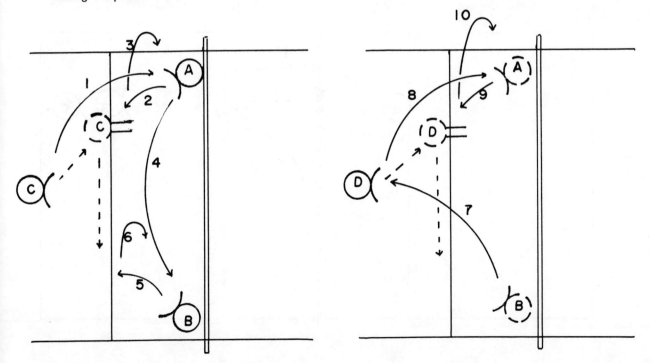

Players A, B, and C start 15 feet apart and close to the net. Players D, E, and F start 15 feet apart and on the back line. The ball is passed or set from A to B to C to D. As each front player receives the ball the back player opposite him must move up as if to cover on the attack. The back player takes the place of the front player after the front player has made the pass. The front player must move to the back line. Keep moving.

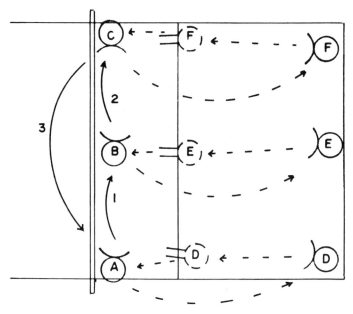

Hang a blanket over the net. Player A throws the balls over the net at random intervals from behind the blanket to various places on the court. The other players take turns starting in back court positions and run to set the ball to a specified target. One player returns balls to A.

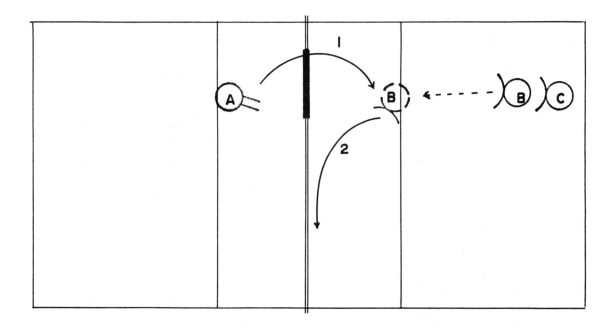

This drill is similar to #130. Player A throws a ball from behind the blanket. Player B must run and pass the ball to C and C sets for D to spike. One player returns the balls to A.

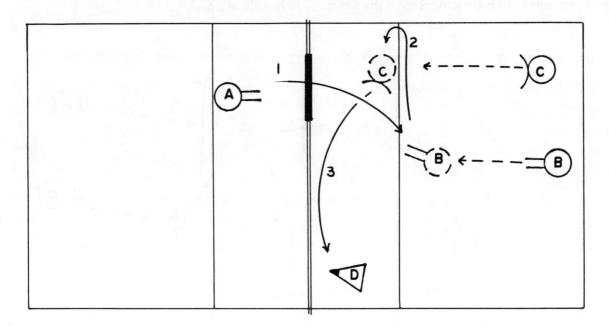

DRILL 132   PASSING, SETTING, SPIKING, BLOCKING   6 PLAYERS, 10 BALLS, BLANKET

The drill is similar to #130. Player A throws a ball from behind the blanket. Player B must pass to C and C sets to D. Player D spikes the ball and E blocks. The sixth player returns balls to A. Repeat the drill as rapidly as possible.

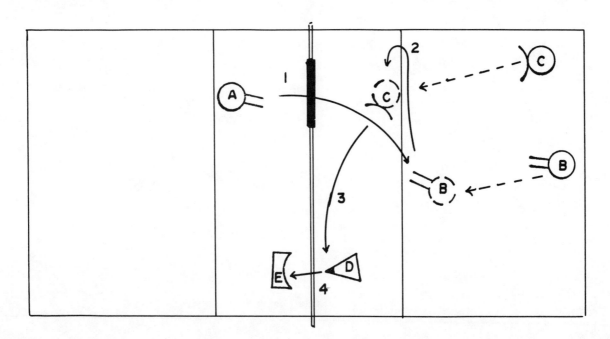

The drill is similar to #130. Player A throws a ball from behind the blanket. Player B must pass the ball to C and C sets for D to spike. Player D spikes the ball directly at E and E digs the ball. The sixth player returns balls to A. Repeat the sequence as rapidly as possible.

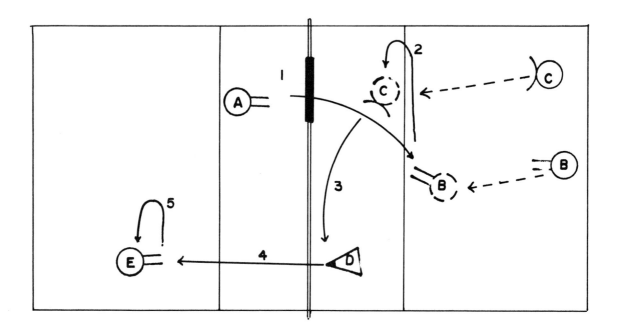

CHAPTER FIVE
SERVING AND RECEIVING DRILLS

Serving and receiving are the two most important skills in volleyball. In recreational volleyball no one else has a chance to play if the serve is out. In competitive volleyball the same is true if the serve is too hard or if the opponents lack skill in receiving. The wise coach and player will spend a great deal of time on these two skills. Small sided games and specific goals should be used to overcome boredom and monotony.

DRILL 134 **SERVING, LEARNING SEQUENCE** 1 PLAYER, 1 BALL

Have the player assume the correct stance for the serve. Have the player mimic the arm and body action and correct any errors. The player next serves to a target on the wall. Start serving from 5 feet away from the wall and move back one step each time the target is hit. Have the player do drill #135. It is probably better to allow the player to serve the ball directly from his hand when learning the underhand and sidearm serves.

DRILL 135 **SERVING** 2 PLAYERS, 1 BALL

Two players serve back and forth to each other over the net. With beginners it is wise to start serving from 15 feet back from the net and gradually move back.

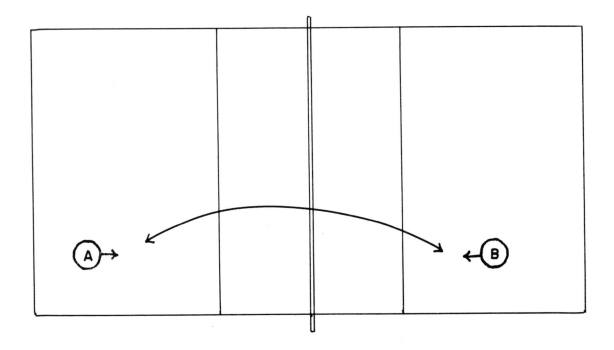

DRILL 136   **SERVING**   1 PLAYER, 1 BALL, 1 CHAIR

Place a chair on the court and serve to hit the chair. Move the chair from place to place.

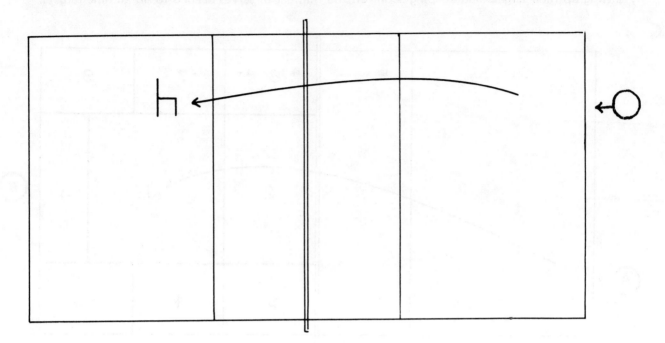

DRILL 137   **SERVING**   1 PLAYER, 1 BALL

Mark a target on the wall 3 feet square and 9 feet above the floor. Serve to the target from a distance of 30 feet. Start beginners closer to the wall and slowly move back.

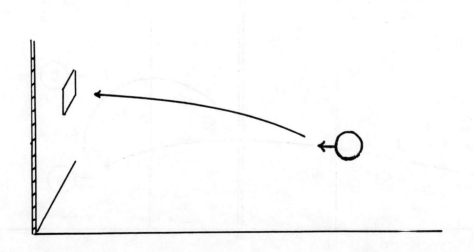

DRILL 138   **SERVING**   2 PLAYERS, 1 BALL

Mark targets on the court and have the player serve to each of the targets in turn. Play 'Serve Golf' by setting up nine targets and keeping score on the number of serves needed to hit all nine targets.

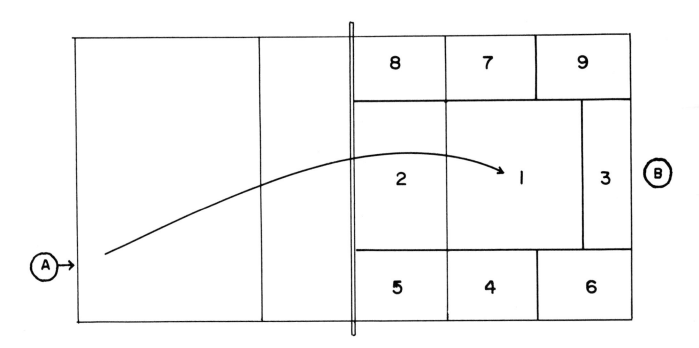

DRILL 139   **SERVING, RECEIVING**   3 PLAYERS, 2 BALLS

One player serves alternately to each of the other two players. The players who are receiving must pass the ball accurately to a target. Use a tumbling mat or a chair as a target.

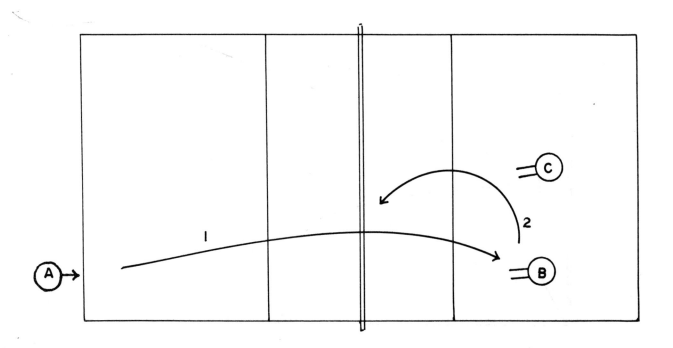

DRILL 140   SERVING, RECEIVING   2 PLAYERS, 1 BALL

One player serves and the other player moves to a different place on the court after each serve. The server must try to hit the receiver with his serve. The receiver passes the ball to a target.

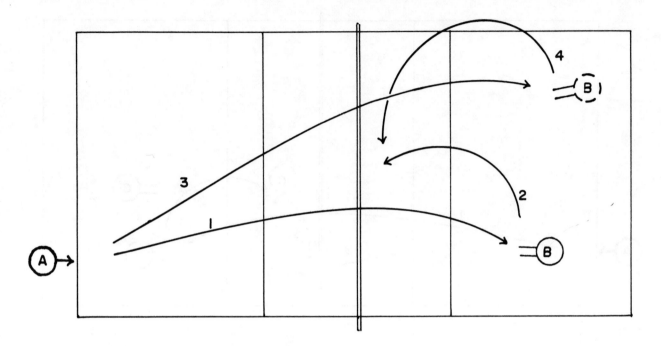

DRILL 141   SERVING, RECEIVING, SETTING   4 PLAYERS, 2 BALLS

One player serves, two players receive, and one player sets. Try to pass the ball accurately to the setter. The player who did not receive the serve moves up to either pass or tip the ball back to the server.

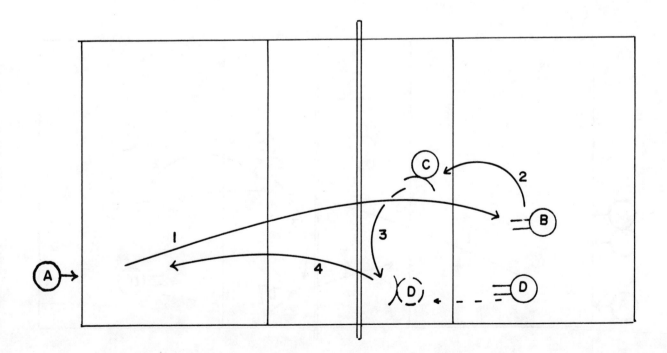

DRILL 142   SERVING, RECEIVING, SETTING, SPIKING   3 PLAYERS, 1 BALL

Player A serves and player B receives. Player B passes to C and C sets for B to spike. Change positions after 10 successful spikes.

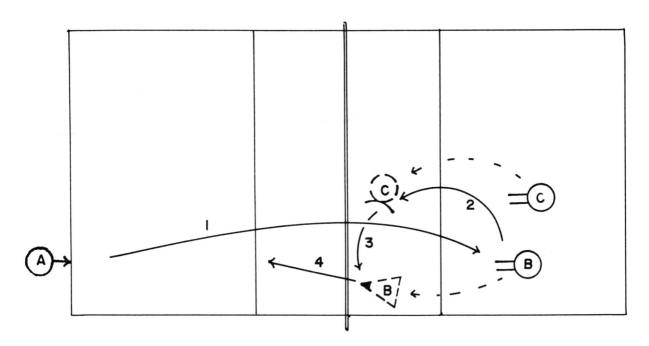

DRILL 143   SERVING, RECEIVING, SETTING, SPIKING   6 PLAYERS, 10 BALLS

Three players alternate serving. Three players set up to receive. One player receives the ball, a second player sets the ball, and the third spikes the ball. All three of the receiving players must make one of the plays on the ball.

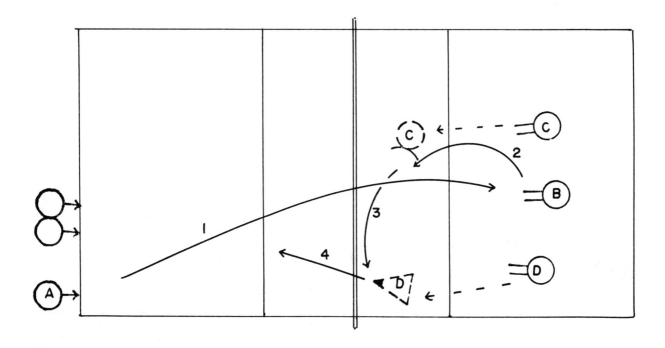

DRILL 144   SERVING, RECEIVING, SETTING, SPIKING   6 PLAYERS, 10 BALLS

Three players alternate serving and the other three players set up to receive the serve. They receive, set and spike. After each attack, the receiving players must run and touch the back line before setting up again.

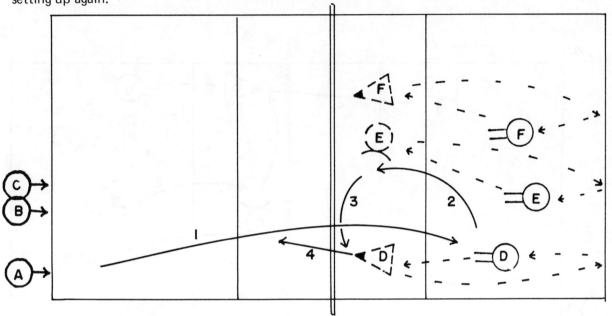

DRILL 145   SERVING, RECEIVING, SETTING, ATTACKING, COVERING   7 PLAYERS, 5 BALLS

One player serves and six players set up to receive. The team receives, sets, and attacks. The players must 'flow' with each play and move to cover. Rotate after 5 successful attacks.

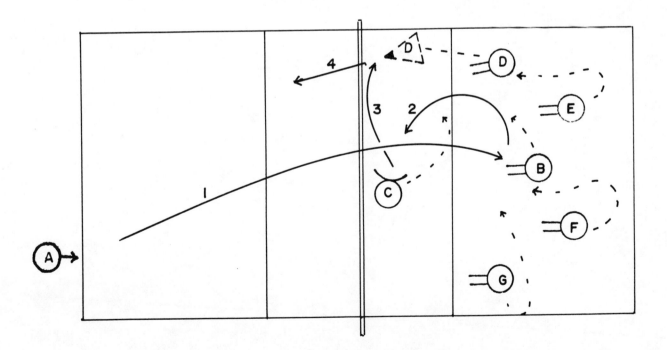

One player serves and six players set up to receive. They must receive, set, and attack towards a target. Change back and front lines after each 10 successful attacking plays.

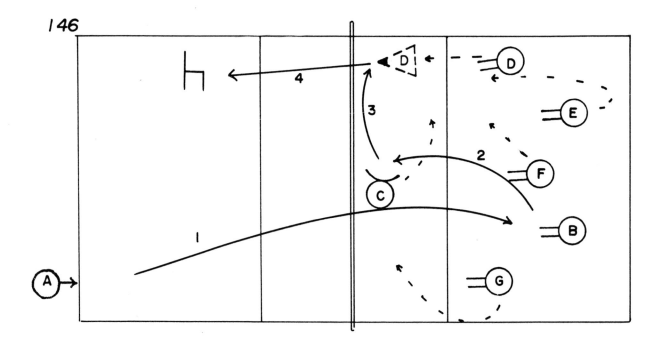

146

CHAPTER SIX
ATTACKING DRILLS

The modern game of "power" volleyball is built around the attack. Hitting a hard spike into court is a thrill for any player. The object of the attack, however, is to score and the soft tip is often as effective as the hard spike. Most of the drills in this chapter are suitable for practicing either the tip or the spike. The first few drills, if used in sequence, can be utilized in teaching spiking to beginners. However, the spike can be learned more efficiently and effectively through the use of an "attacker" volleyball (a ball suspended on surgical rubber tubing). The "attacker" volleyball is manufactured in Japan and available from most dealers.

DRILL 147   **SPIKING**   **1 PLAYER, 1 BALL**

The player starts 15 feet away from a wall. The ball is held up high with the left hand and then hit with the right hand. Hit the ball so that it bounces on the floor and then the wall. Be sure that the ball is held in front of the hitting shoulder and that the wind up and action of the hitting arm is correct. This drill is for beginners and for warming up.

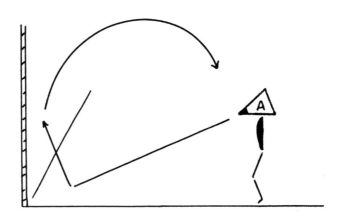

DRILL 148   **SPIKING**   **1 PLAYER, 1 BALL**

The player starts 15 feet away from a wall. The ball is thrown up, or bounced high on the floor. The player jumps and spikes the ball to the floor and wall. Catch the ball and repeat.

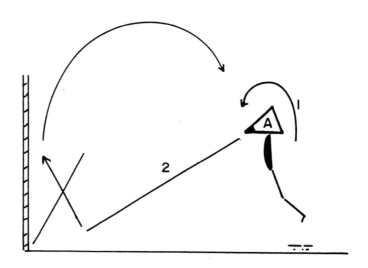

DRILL 149   **SPIKING**   1 PLAYER, 1 BALL

The player runs in toward the net, throws the ball up so that it rises about 2 feet above the net. He jumps and spikes the ball. This is a very quick action drill.

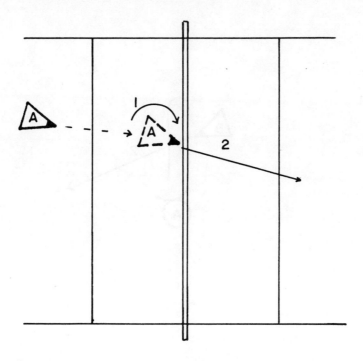

DRILL 150   **SPIKING**   2 PLAYERS, 1 BALL, TABLE

One player stands on a table and holds the ball above the net. The other player jumps and spikes the ball. This drill is for beginners.

DRILL 151   **SPIKING**   2 PLAYERS, 1 BALL

One player throws the ball up carefully for an ideal set. The other player jumps and spikes the ball. Concentrate on correct technique.

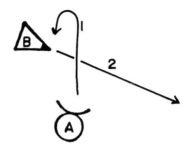

DRILL 152   **SPIKING**   2 PLAYERS, 1 BALL

Two players start on opposite sides of the net. One player throws a ball high over the net. The other player jumps and spikes the ball back at the first player.

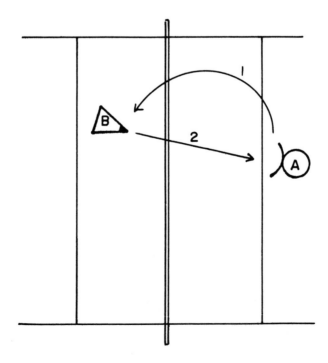

DRILL 153   **SETTING, SPIKING**   2 PLAYERS, 1 BALL

Player A throws a ball carefully to the setter. The second player sets the ball for A to spike. With beginners, be sure that the throw to the setter is a good one to make it easy to set.

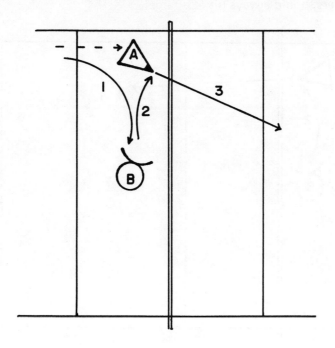

DRILL 154   **SETTING, SPIKING**   3 PLAYERS, 5 BALLS

Player A passes or throws a ball to B and B sets for C to spike. This drill can be used with different types of sets. Rotate after 5 spikes.

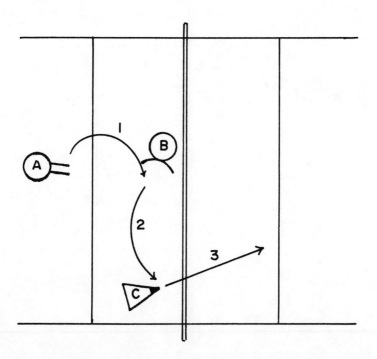

DRILL 155   SETTING, SPIKING   2 PLAYERS, 1 BALL, CHAIR

Player A passes to B and B sets for A to spike. Player A attempts to hit a chair or other target. Progress from hitting towards the opposite back corner, to hitting down the line, to hitting a sharp angle. Intermediate players should always hit at a target.

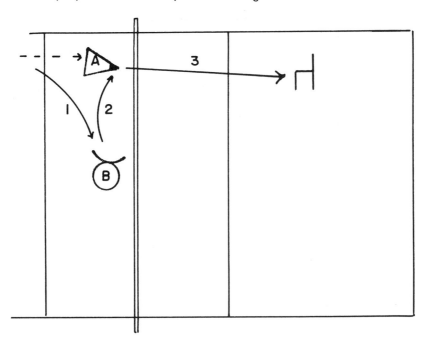

DRILL 156   SPIKING   4—10 PLAYERS, 4—10 BALLS, COACH

The coach starts close to the net. The players start in a line behind the attack line. The player throws his ball low and at waist height to the coach and then runs in and jumps to spike. As or slightly after the player jumps the coach throws the ball up to the spiker's hand so the spiker can hit the ball. The spiker should be in the air waiting for the ball on this drill. Keep moving rapidly.

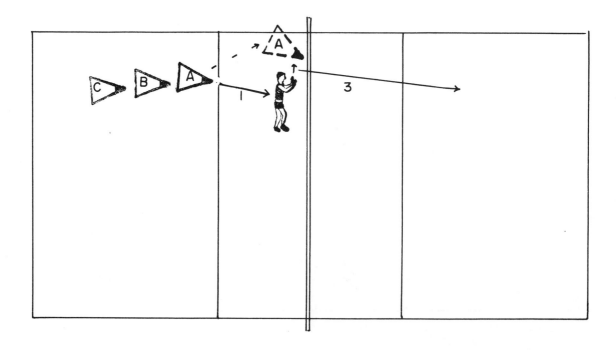

DRILL 157 **SPIKING, COVERING** **TEAM, 10 BALLS**

One player sets and the others take turns spiking. The second player in line passes a ball to the setter and the first player in line spikes the ball. The second player moves to cover behind the spiker.

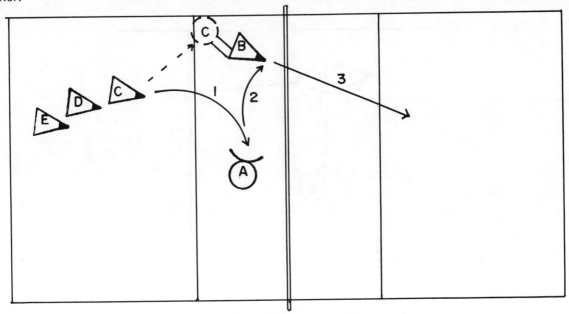

DRILL 158 **SPIKING** **3 PLAYERS, 15 — 20 BALLS**

Players A and C start 10 feet apart and close to the net. Player B starts between them and 6 feet back from the net. Players A and C alternate throwing or setting balls for B to spike. Player B must alternate hitting with his left hand and then his right hand.

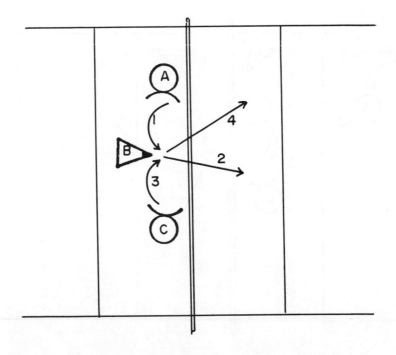

The spiker starts with his back to the net. The other player throws the ball up for an ideal set and the spiker jumps and turns and spikes the ball. Be sure that the spiker turns completely before hitting the ball.

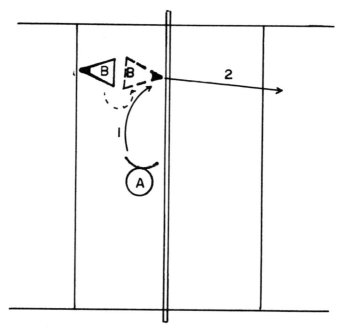

Player A passes to B and B sets for C to spike. As C jumps, A yells either "line" or "angle" and C must spike down the line or angle. Repeat.

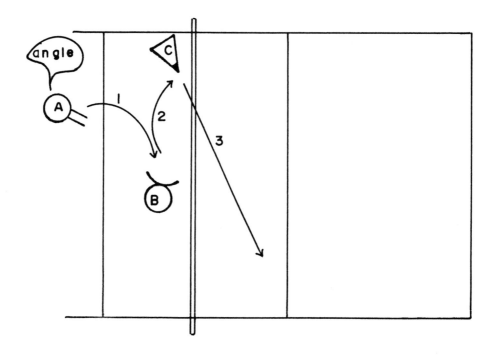

DRILL 161 **SETTING, SPIKING** **3 PLAYERS, 2 BALLS**

Player A passes to B and B sets for C to spike. As C jumps, A yells either "right" OR "left" and C must hit with his right or left hand.

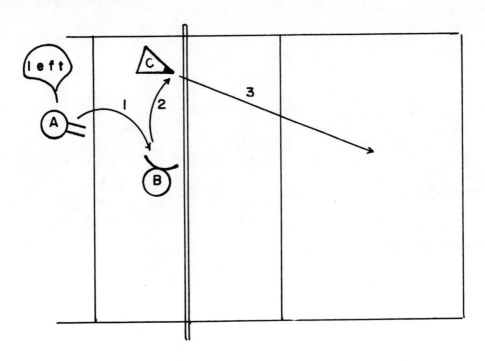

DRILL 162 **SETTING, SPIKING** **4 PLAYERS, 15 BALLS**

Player A throws a ball to B close to one side-line and B sets for C to spike from the middle. Player A then throws a ball to D close to the other side-line and D sets for C to spike. Keep moving rapidly.

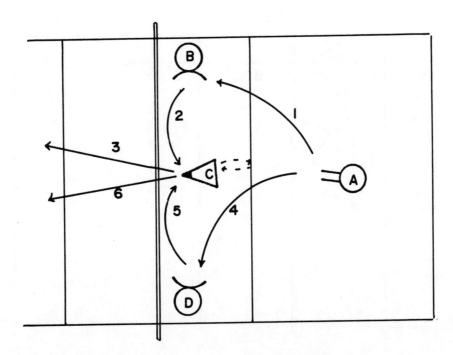

The player starts 5 feet away from a wall. He passes the ball to the wall using a face pass, jumps and tips the ball to the wall. Continue.

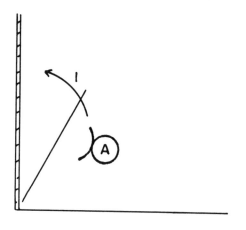
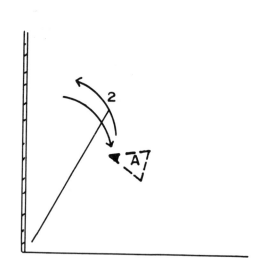

DRILL 164   SETTING, ATTACKING   3 PLAYERS, 15 BALLS, 1 CHAIR

Player A throws or passes to B and B sets for C to spike. The first ball is set to the tape and C spikes down the line. The second ball is set to the middle and C must tip to a target. The third ball is set to the tape and the fourth to the middle. Continue rapidly.

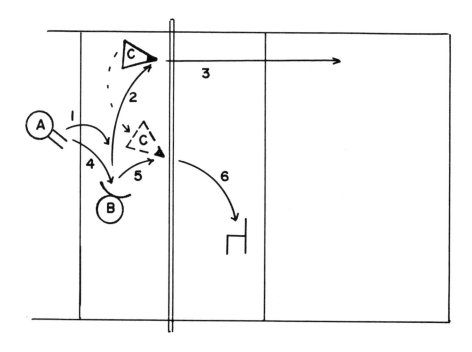

DRILL 165   SPIKING, DIVING   2 PLAYERS, 10 BALLS

Player A sets 3 consecutive balls for B to spike and then throws a fourth ball into the court behind B. Player B must turn and dive to recover the ball. Player A then sets a fifth ball for B to spike. Rest and repeat.

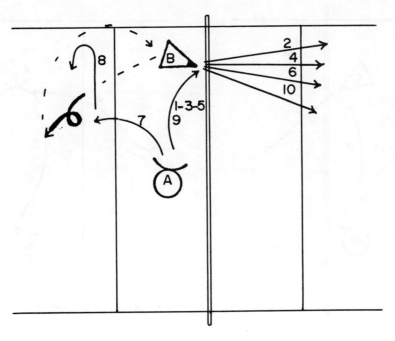

DRILL 166   SETTING, SPIKING   7 PLAYERS, 15 BALLS

Player A throws the balls to the setters. Three players, B, C, and D start 15 feet apart and close to the net as setters. Three other players start as spikers. The balls are thrown to B, C and D in rapid succession and the three spikers move to spike with their respective setters.

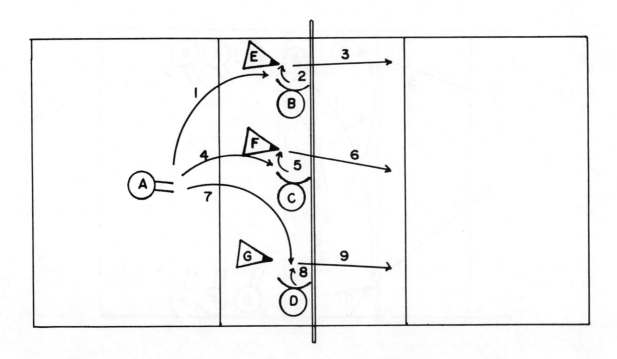

DRILL 167 **SETTING, SPIKING** 3 PLAYERS, 10 BALLS

Player A throws balls alternately to B and C. Player B sets for C to spike and C sets for B to spike. Continue rapidly and rotate after 10 hits.

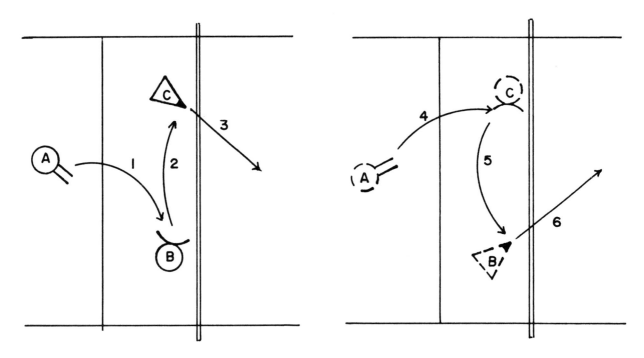

DRILL 168 **SETTING, SPIKING** 8 PLAYERS, 7 BALLS

The players start in two lines on each side of the court. Player A starts the drill by setting across court for B to spike. As soon as B spikes, C throws a ball for B to set and B sets across court for C to spike. Continue. Each player must set immediately after he spikes. The players chase their balls and move to the end of the other line.

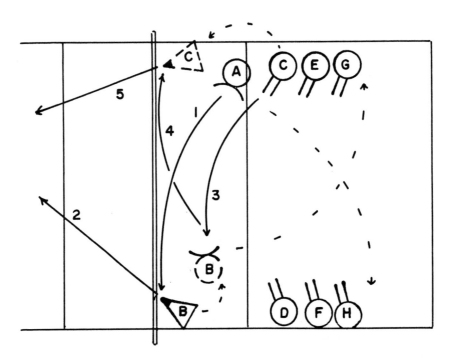

DRILL 169   PASSING, SETTING, SPIKING   4 PLAYERS, 15 BALLS

Player A starts on one side of the net and the other three players start on the other side. Player A throws the first ball over the net to B and B passes to C and C sets for D to spike. As soon as D spikes, A throws a new ball to D and D passes to B and B sets for C to spike. Player A then throws the next ball over the net to C and C passes to D and D sets for B to spike. Continue rapidly rotating from passer to setter to spiker. A variation is to rotate from spiker to setter to passer.

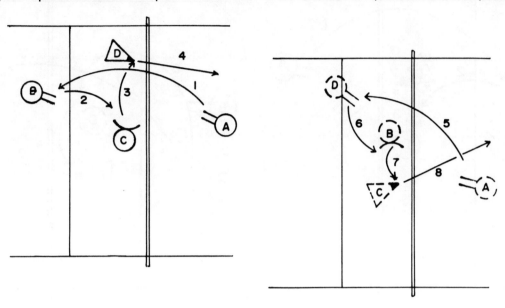

DRILL 170   PASSING, SETTING, SPIKING   6 PLAYERS, 15 BALLS

Player A starts on one side of the net and the other players start on the other side of the net. Player B is the setter and starts close to the net. Players C and E start at the attack line and close to one side-line and D and F start at the attack line and close to the other side-line. Player A throws the ball to the centre of the court and the spiker, C, must move and pass the ball to the setter and then move back towards the side-line to spike the ball. The ball is set high and close to the side-line.

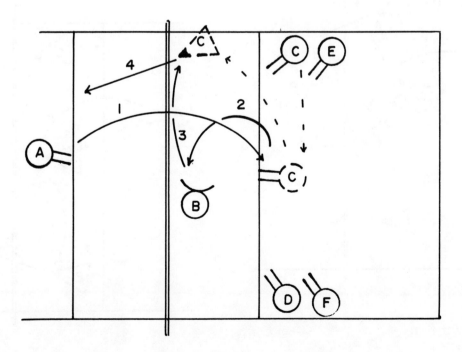

Player A starts on one side of the net and three players start on the other side. Player A throws the ball over the net alternately to B and C. Player B passes to D and D sets either forward or backward. Players B and C criss-cross as they move in to spike. Keep moving rapidly.

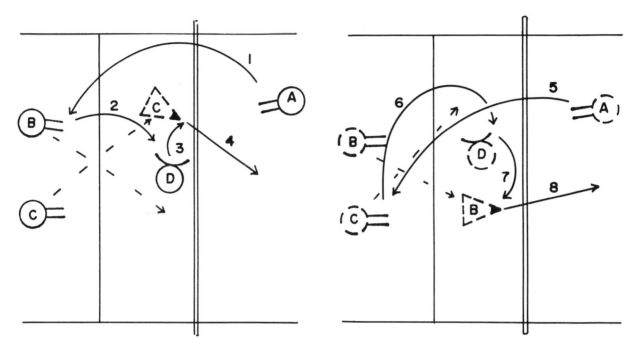

Player A throws or passes the ball to B and B randomly sets the balls to each of three spikers who all move forward to make the attack. The spikers must move back and get ready rapidly. Keep the drill moving.

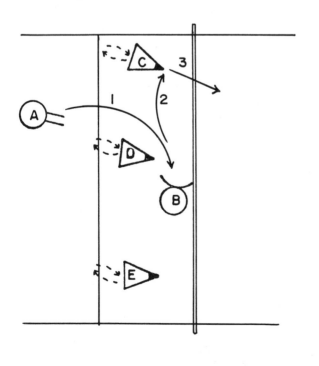
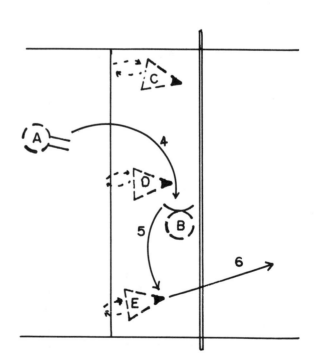

DRILL 173   **SETTING, SPIKING**   **3 PLAYERS, 15 BALLS**

Player A throws or passes to B and B sets for C to spike. The first set is close to the left side-line, the second set is in the middle, and the third set is close to the right side-line. The fourth ball is set in the middle. Continue back and forth across the net.

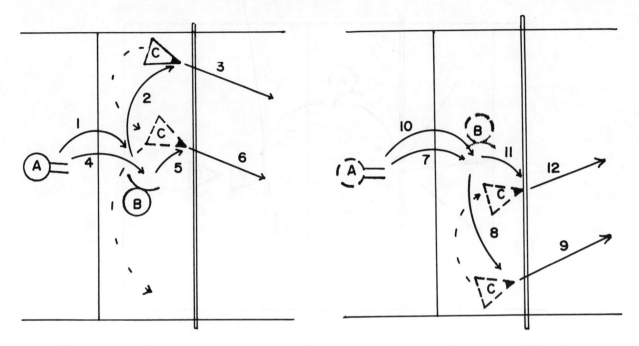

DRILL 174   **SETTING, SPIKING**   **7 PLAYERS, 15 BALLS**

Player A throws the balls to the setters. Three players start close to the net and 15 feet apart as setters. The balls are thrown to the setters in order from B to C to D. Player E will hit each of the 3 sets starting from the side, then the middle, and then the other side. Keep moving rapidly. As soos as one spiker finishes the next starts.

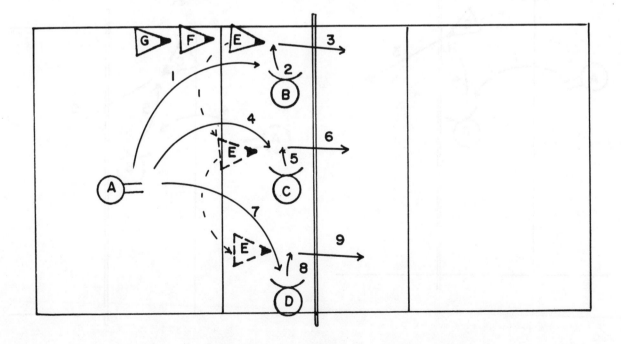

Player A sets and B and C alternate spiking. The spikers use a different angle of approach each time they spike and spike in the direction of their approach. The ball is passed from the spiker to the setter to begin the drill.

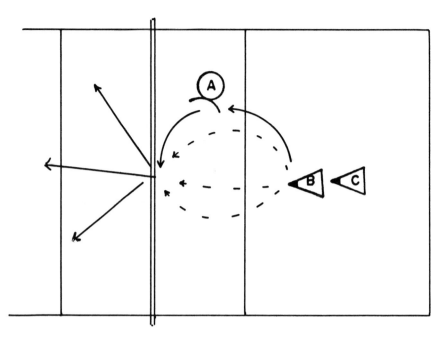

DRILL 176   **SETTING, SPIKING**   3 PLAYERS, 15 BALLS

Player A throws a ball to B and B sets for C to spike. The first ball is set close to the net and the second ball is set back from the net forcing the spiker to move back to spike the ball. Continue rapidly.

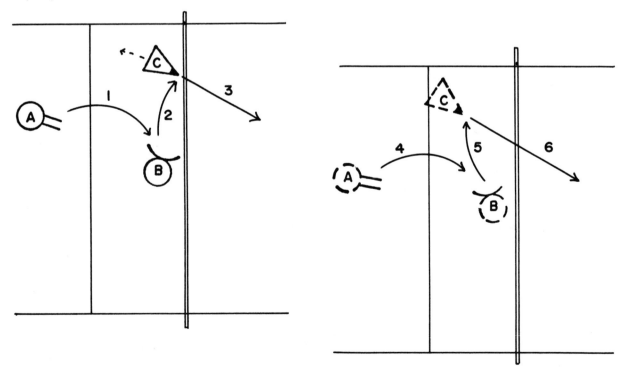

DRILL 177 **SPIKING** 2 PLAYERS, 15 BALLS

Player A throws the balls up in rapid succession for B to spike. The first ball is hit hard to the opposite back corner. The second ball is hit soft. The third ball is hit hard down the line, and the fourth is hit soft. The fifth ball is hit hard down the angle. Continue.

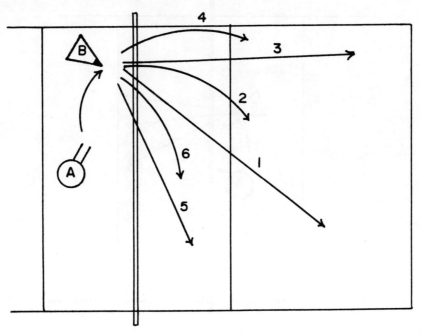

DRILL 178 **SPIKING** 2 PLAYERS, 10 BALLS

Player A throws the balls up in rapid succession for B to spike. Each ball is thrown one foot further away from the net until the player is spiking from the attack line. A variation is to move forward on each spike.

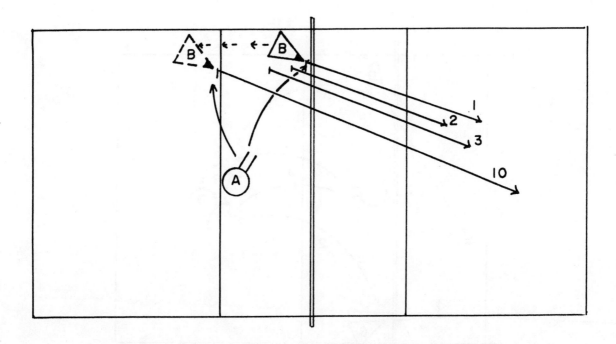

DRILL 179 SPIKING 2 PLAYERS, 20 BALLS

Player A throws the balls up and close to the net in rapid succession. Player B must jump and spike each ball. Other players may be used to retrieve balls and protect against balls rolling under the spiker's feet. This drill is good for conditioning.

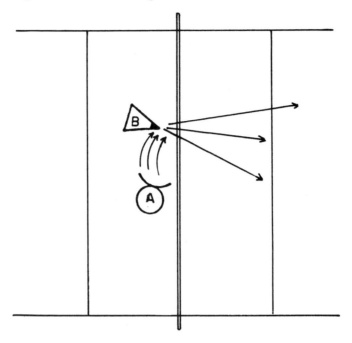

DRILL 180 SETTING, SPIKING 4 PLAYERS, 10 BALLS

Player A starts close to the net and B starts in the centre of the court. Two players alternate spiking from each side. Player A passes to B and B alternates setting to the left front and the right front. The spikers should practice hitting down the line and the angle.

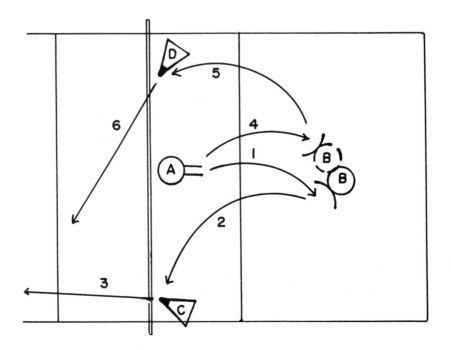

Player A starts in the back left corner. Player B starts in the back right corner. Player C starts in the front left corner. Player A passes to B and B sets for C to spike. Practice hitting down the angle first and then practice hitting down the line. Keep the sets high.

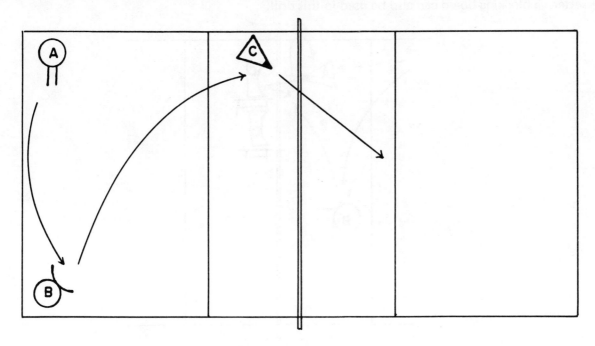

DRILL 182   SETTING, SPIKING   3 PLAYERS, 10 BALLS

Player C starts on one side of the net close to the attack line. Player A passes to B and B sets for A to spike. As player A jumps to spike, C moves to his left or right. Player A must hit the ball in the other direction away from C.

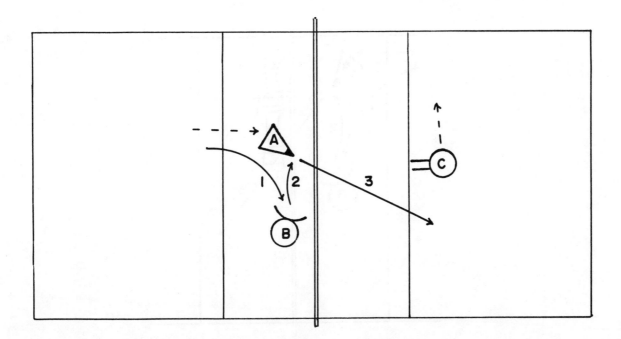

DRILL 183   **SETTING, SPIKING, RECOVERING**   4 PLAYERS, 10 BALLS,
                                                                          2 TABLES

Two players stand on tables close to the net and block. A third player sets the ball and a fourth
player spikes into the blocker's hands. The spiker attempts to dig the blocked ball back up to the
setter. A blocking board can also be used in this drill.

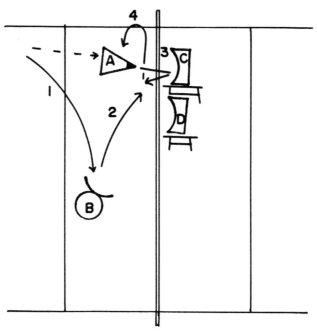

DRILL 184   **SETTING, SPIKING**   4 PLAYERS, 10 BALLS, 2 TABLES

Two players stand on tables close to the net and attempt to block the ball. Player A passes to B and
B sets for A to spike. The spiker must attempt to spike around the block into court. A blocking
board can also be used.

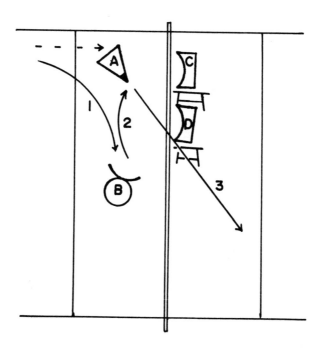

Player A passes to B and B sets for A to spike while C and D block. Player C and D move their hands before the spike to leave either a hole in the block or room for the spiker to hit around the block. The spiker must look and then hit. This is an advanced drill.

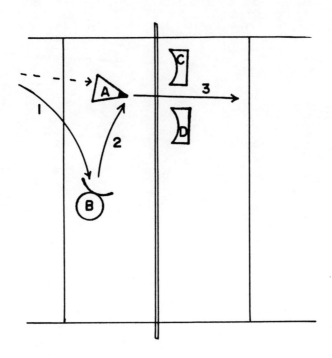

CHAPTER SEVEN
BLOCKING DRILLS

Theoretically a team need only serve and block to score points. Although the spike is the most spectacular way of scoring, the block is the more effective. Unfortunately the development of blocking skills depends upon decent spiking. There will, therefore, be a lag between the effectiveness of the block and the effectiveness of the attack. However, everytime a ball is spiked in practice an opportunity is provided for another player to develop his blocking skills. It is up to the coach and the player to take advantage of this opportunity. The drills in this chapter range from those to be used in learning the basic skill to those used in the refinement of advanced techniques.

DRILL 186 BLOCKING 1 PLAYER, 1 WALL

The player stands one foot away from a wall with the hands held at shoulder height. He squats and jumps to touch the wall as high as he can with both hands. This is a drill for beginners and encourages bringing the hands up close to the body.

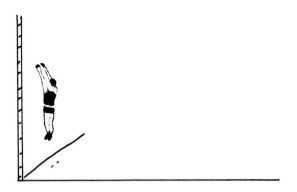

DRILL 187 BLOCKING 1 PLAYER, COACH, 1 BALL, TABLE

The coach stands on a table and holds a ball over the net or above the height of the net on his side. The player starts close to the net, squats and jumps to push the ball down as if blocking using both hands. This is a drill for beginners.

DRILL 188   BLOCKING   1 PLAYER, COACH, 1 BALL, TABLE

The coach stands on a table and holds a ball above the height of the net. The player jumps to block the ball. As he jumps the coach moves the ball to the left or the right and the player attempts to reach and block the ball or push it down with both hands.

DRILL 189   BLOCKING   1 PLAYER, COACH, 2 BALLS, TABLE

The coach stands on a table and holds two balls above the height of the net and about 18 inches apart. The player jumps and pushes one ball and then the other using both hands and simulating the proper blocking action.

DRILL 190 **BLOCKING** 2 PLAYERS, 1 BALL

The players start on opposite sides of the net. Player A throws the ball low over the net. Player B jumps and blocks the ball. This drill can also be done by having the player throw the ball into the blocker's hands after he has jumped. This drill is for beginners.

DRILL 191 **BLOCKING** 2 PLAYERS, 1 BALL

The players start on opposite sides of the net. Player B jumps to block and player A throws the ball low over the net and slightly to B's left or right. The blocker must reach to the side to block the ball.

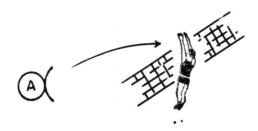

DRILL 192 **BLOCKING** 12 PLAYERS, 6 BALLS, 6 CHAIRS

Six players stand on chairs on one side of the net. They each hold a ball above the net. The other players move sideways along the net and jump and try to push each ball down as if they were blocking. Move to the end of the line and start again. Try not to touch the net.

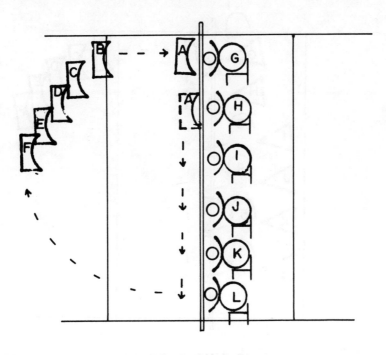

DRILL 193 **BLOCKING** 12 PLAYERS, 6 BALLS

Six players start on one side of the net each with a ball. The other six players take turns moving sideways along the net. They must jump and block each ball as the players on the other side throw the balls low over the net.

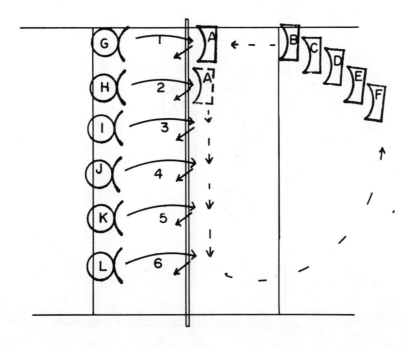

DRILL 194   **BLOCKING**   12 PLAYERS, 6 BALLS

Six players start on one side of the net each with a ball. These players throw the ball up, jump, and spike it straight ahead over the net. The other six players take turns moving sideways along the net and attempt to block each ball in succession.

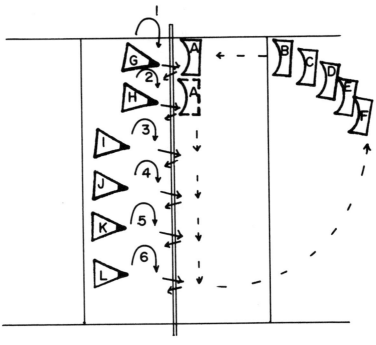

DRILL 195   **SETTING, SPIKING, BLOCKING**   3 PLAYERS, 1 BALL

Player A passes to B and B sets for A to spike while C blocks. Player A must spike into the blocker's hands. This drill is primarily for the blocker's benefit.

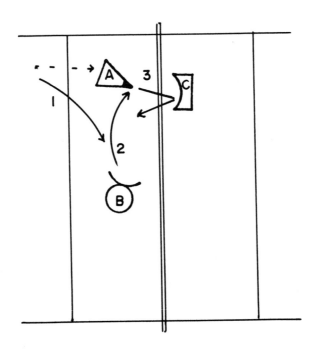

DRILL 196   SETTING, SPIKING, BLOCKING   3 PLAYERS, 5 BALLS

Player A passes to B and B sets to different places on the net for A to spike. Player C must move the block. The ball should be set fairly close to the net to give the blocker the advantage.

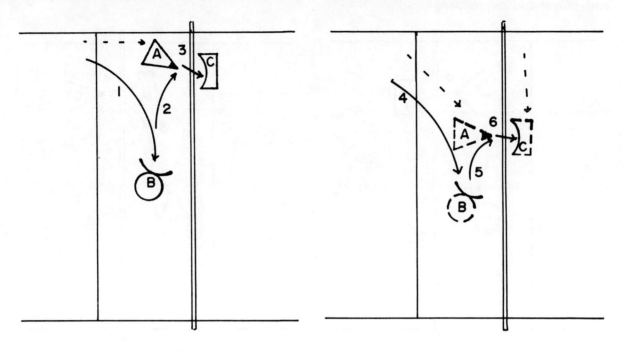

DRILL 197   SPIKING, BLOCKING, SETTING   3 PLAYERS, 10 BALLS

Players B and C start on opposite sides of the net. Player A throws the ball up randomly to B or to C. If B receives the pass he may either (a) spike the ball, or (b) SET THE BALL' Player C must block. The same applies to C if he receives the pass.

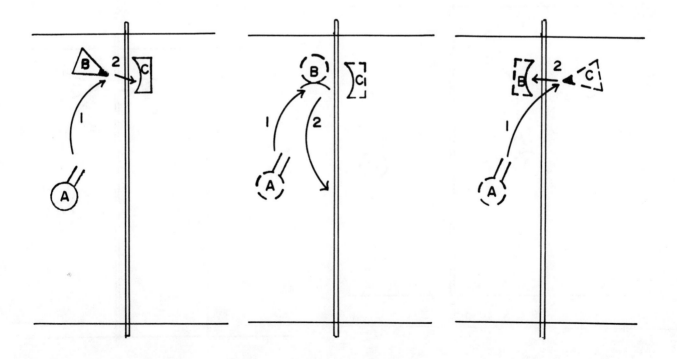

DRILL 198   **SPIKING, BLOCKING**   3 PLAYERS, 10 BALLS

Two players start on opposite sides of the net and 3 feet back from the net. The third player throws a ball up for one of the players to spike. The other player must block. Throw the balls randomly to each player and keep moving rapidly.

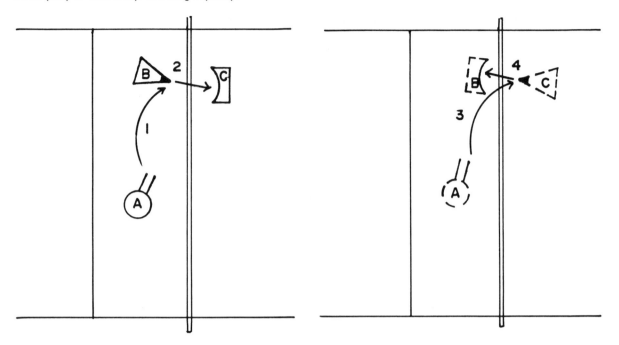

DRILL 199   **SPIKING, BLOCKING**   4 PLAYERS, 10 BALLS

Two players start on each side of the net. One player on each side throws the balls and the other either spikes or blocks. Player A throws for B to spike and then C throws for D to spike. Player B must block D and D must block B.

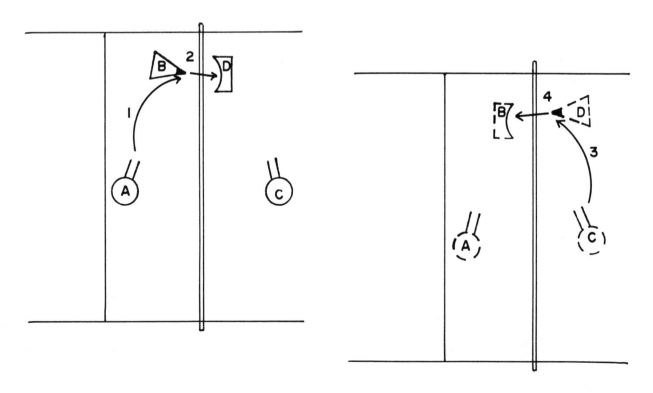

DRILL 200 **SETTING, SPIKING, BLOCKING** **8 PLAYERS, 10 BALLS**

Four players start as blockers with two of them blocking. After each spike, one of the two blockers moves out of the block and a new player moves in to block. One player sets and the other three players alternate spiking. Keep moving as fast as possible.

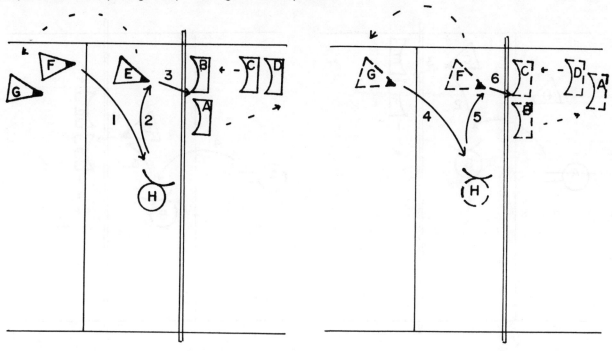

DRILL 201 **SETTING, SPIKING, BLOCKING** **4 PLAYERS, 10 BALLS**

Player A passes to B and B sets for A to spike while C and D block. One of the blockers starts in the middle and moves out to block each time. Rotate after 10 balls have been blocked. It may be necessary to tie a ribbon to the net and have the middle blocker hold the ribbon until the set is made.

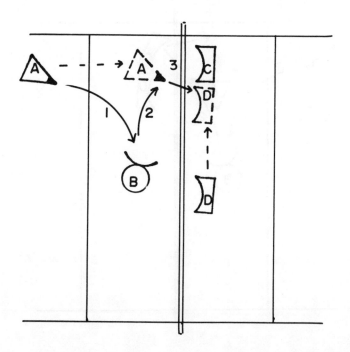

DRILL 202 **SETTING, SPIKING, BLOCKING** **6 PLAYERS, 15 BALLS**

Two players start blocking. Player A throws the balls to the setter and the other two players alternate spiking. The setter moves backward across the net and places each set 3 feet to the right of the previous set. Keep moving rapidly.

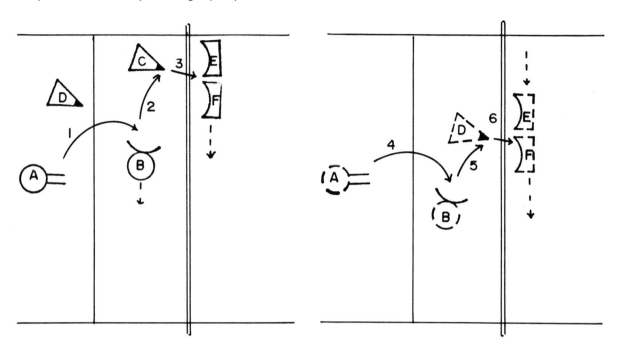

DRILL 203 **SETTING, SPIKING, BLOCKING** **4 PLAYERS, 5 BALLS**

Player A passes to B and B sets close to the net and player A spikes while C and D block. The spiker attempts to "brush off" of the block or to hit out of bounds off of the block. The blockers attempt to turn the spiked ball back into court. This is an advanced drill.

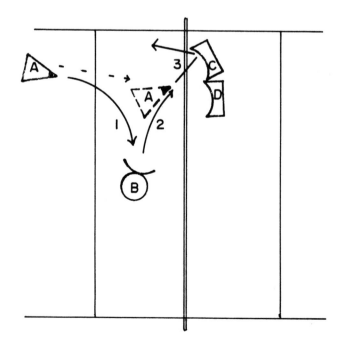

Three players start blocking. The setter alternates setting to each side forcing the middle blocker to move from side to side to block. The other players spike from the sides. Rotate when the middle blocker is tired. This is a good conditioning drill.

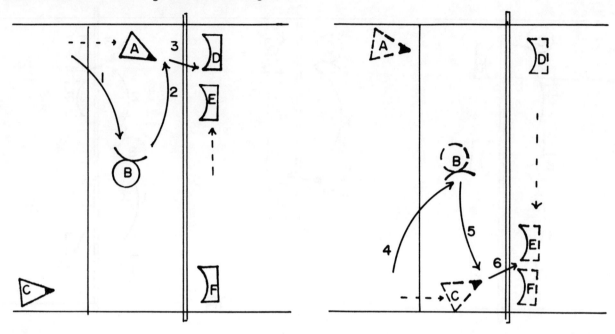

DRILL 205   SETTING, SPIKING, BLOCKING   8 PLAYERS, 10 BALLS

Players F, G and H start blocking. Players C, D and E start spiking. Player A throws a ball to B and B sets either a regular high set to one of the two outside spikers or a low set to the middle spiker. The setter sets randomly to either side or the middle. The blockers always try to put up a two-man block at the side and a three-man block in the middle. Rotate or change blockers after 10 successful blocks.

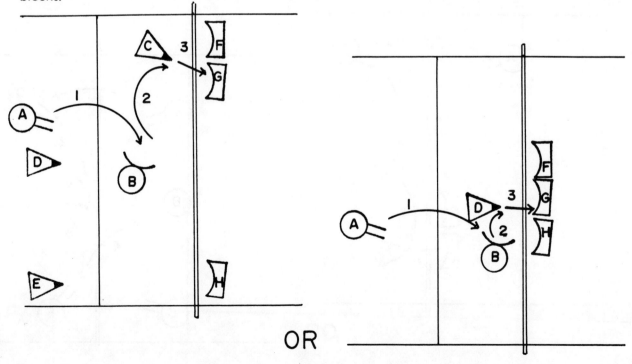

OR

121

DRILL 206 SETTING, SPIKING, BLOCKING 6 PLAYERS, 1 BALL

Three players start on one side of the net as blockers. The other three players start on the other side of the net and pass the ball along the net. These players may either spike the ball or set it to the next player. They try to catch the blockers by surprise. They should fake a spike every time and should spike at least once every 5 passes.

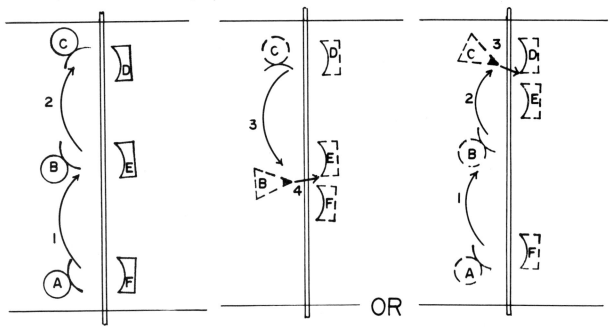

OR

DRILL 207 PASSING, SETTING, SPIKING, BLOCKING 6 PLAYERS, 1 BALL

Three players start on each side of the net. The ball is passed over the net and the three players may either (a) pass, set and spike, or (b) pass, set and pass the ball over the net. If they spike, the players on the other side must block. If they pass, the other team must stay down. Continue rapidly.

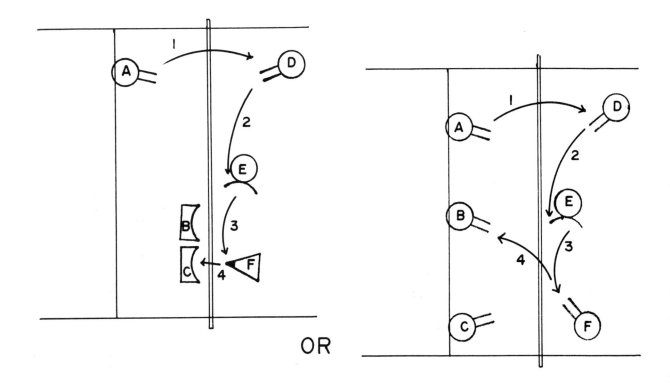

OR

DRILL 208   **SETTING, SPIKING, BLOCKING, DIGGING   4 PLAYERS, 10 BALLS**

Player A passes to B and B sets for A to spike while C blocks. As soon as A spikes, D throws a ball over the net to the side of C. Player C must land, crouch and turn, and dig the second ball high to a target.

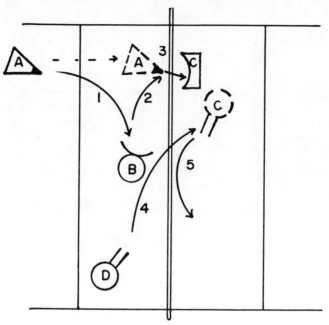

DRILL 209   **SETTING, SPIKING, BLOCKING, NET RECOVERY**   4 PLAYERS, 10 BALLS

Player A passes to B and B sets for A to spike while C blocks. After each attempt to block, player D throws a ball into the net beside C as if the ball had rebounded from a back row player. The blocker must either set the ball or bump it over the net.

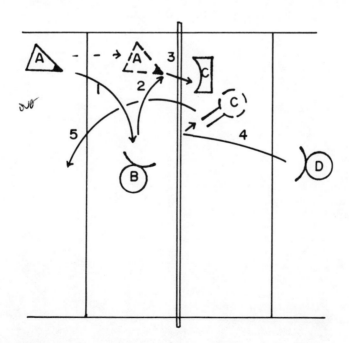

CHAPTER EIGHT
BACK COURT DEFENSIVE DRILLS

In power volleyball there are two lines of defense — the blockers and the back court players. If a player can properly read the play and anticipate where the attacker will hit the ball he need never hit the floor. Unfortunately this concept seems to be merely theoretical. Players must learn to dive and to roll to make the play on the ball. The method of landing needs to be practiced so that the player can avoid injury and recover rapidly to get back into the game. Many players tend to emphasize the style of the roll or dive rather than the trajectory of the ball after they play it. Coaches should be sure to emphasize the high accurate pass when using the drills in this chapter.

DRILL 210   **SPIKING, DIGGING**   **2 PLAYERS, 1 BALL**

Player A jumps and spikes the ball at B. Player B digs the ball. This is normally a warm up drill. Using a jump simulates the angle of attack that would occur in a game.

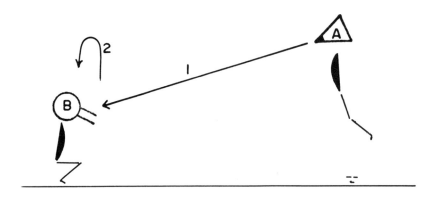

DRILL 211   **PASSING, SPIKING, DIGGING**   **3 PLAYERS, 1 BALL**

Three players start a triangle about 10 feet apart. Player A passes to B and B spikes at C. Player C digs or bumps the ball to A. The spiking must be accurate and shoudl be half speed to ensure control.

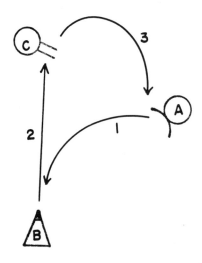

Three players start in a triangle about 10 feet apart. Player A throws the ball up to himself and spikes at B. Player B digs or bumps the ball to C. Player C passes the ball to himself and spikes at A. Player A bumps to B. Continue.

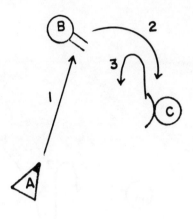

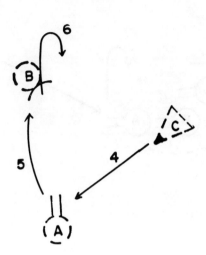

DRILL 213   SPIKING, DIGGING   5—6 PLAYERS, 5—10 BALLS

Four players start in a square about 15 feet apart. Players A and C spike and B and D dig. Player A throws the ball up and hits at B. Player B must bump the ball to C. Player C passes to himself and hits at D. Player D must bump to A. Continue. One or two other players collect and feed balls to A and C when necessary. The object is to dig the ball out on an angle to a target. The person digging should concentrate on proper feet alignment and body position.

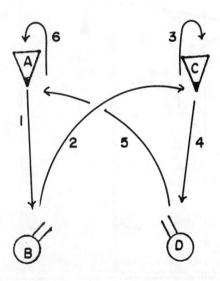

DRILL 214   DIGGING, DIVING OR ROLLING

The coach stands on a table about 20 feet in front of a line of five players. The coach spikes or tips a ball at each player in rapid succession. The players must dig the ball up high towards a target. The coach should force each player to extend himself. The other five players chase balls and hand them to the coach and later take their turn in line.

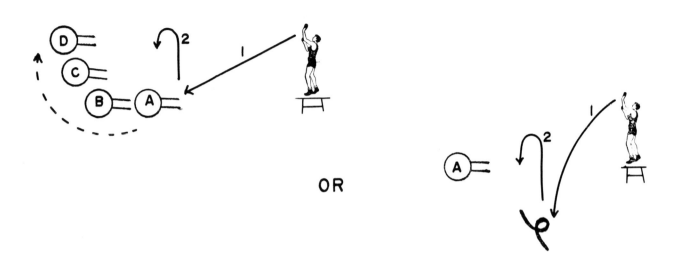

OR

DRILL 215   DIGGING, SETTING   6 PLAYERS, COACH, 15 BALLS

The coach stands on a table on one side of the net. Three players assume back court positions on the other side of the net. The other three players gather balls and hand them to the coach. The coach spikes or tips the ball to one of the three back court players. They must dig the ball and a second player must then set the ball to a target. All three must then run back and touch the back line and move into position for the next ball. Keep moving rapidly.

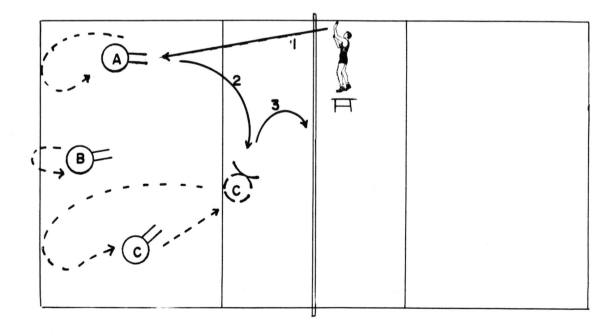

DRILL 216   DIGGING, DIVING OR ROLLING   5 PLAYERS, COACH, 15 BALLS

One player starts at one end of the gym and the coach starts about 15 feet in front of him. The coach throws a ball to a spot in front and to the side of the player forcing him to dive or roll as he digs the ball. The coach moves backwards down the floor throwing balls in front of the player as he follows him down the floor. The other four players recover loose balls and hand them to the coach. Each player takes his turn diving and rolling. It would be wise to use padding on this drill.

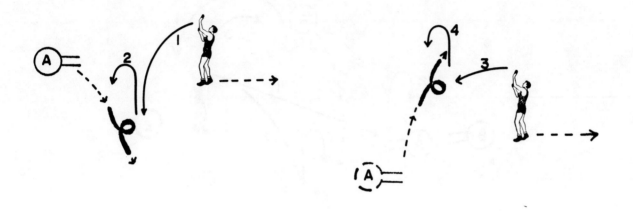

DRILL 217   DIGGING, SPIKING   4 PLAYERS, 10 BALLS

Three players start about 10 feet apart in a line. A fourth player, A, starts opposite the middle player, B. Player A throws a ball up and B jumps, turns, and spikes at C. Player C digs the ball. Player A then throws a second ball and B jumps, turns, and spikes the ball at D. Player D digs the ball. Continue.

DRILL 218   DIGGING, SETTING, DIVING OR ROLLING   5 PLAYERS, COACH,
                                                                15 BALLS

The coach stands on one side of the court and the players start in a line on the other side of the
court. The coach either spikes or tips the balls in rapid succession to the players. The players must
play 3 balls in a row and then move to the end of the line. They must dig or bump the first ball, run
and set the second ball, and dig the third ball using a dive or a roll. The coach should force the
players to extend themselves on this drill. One player feeds balls to the coach.

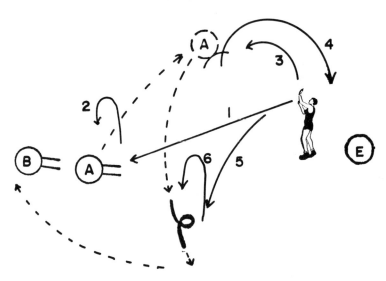

DRILL 219   DIGGING, DIVING OR ROLLING, SETTING   5 PLAYERS, COACH,
                                                                15 BALLS

The coach stands on a table on one side of the net. He tips the ball over the net forcing either B or
C to dive or roll when digging the ball. Player A must move under the pass and set the ball to a
target. The other players return balls and feed them to the coach. Keep tipping alternately to B and
C as fast as possible. Player A must set every ball.

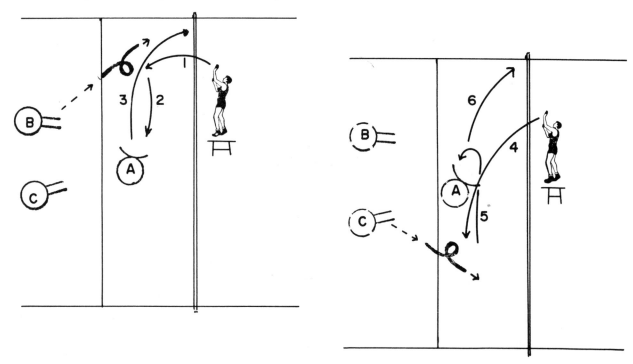

130

DRILL 220　　　　　DIGGING, DIVING OR ROLLING　　　6 PLAYERS, 10 BALLS

Players A, B and C stand at the net and 10 feet apart. Players D and E start on the back line and move forward to play the ball alternately as it is hit or tipped by one of the net players. They must dive or roll when necessary and then rush back to the back line. A sixth player feeds balls to A, B and C.

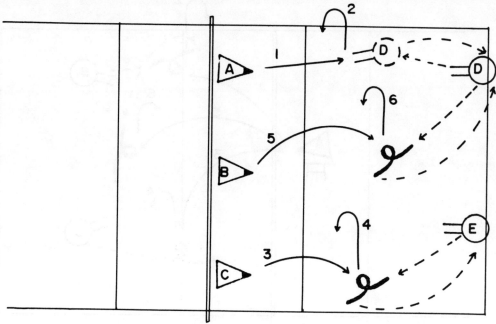

DRILL 221　　　　DIGGING, DIVING OR ROLLING, SETTING　3 PLAYERS, 15 BALLS

Players B and C start about 10 feet apart and 20 feet back from the net. Player A starts at the net and either hits or tips the ball to either B or C. Player B or C digs the ball and the other moves in to set the ball to a target. Players B and C then move back rapidly to their places and A hits the ball at the other player. Force the players to extend themselves when they dive or roll by properly placing the tipped balls.

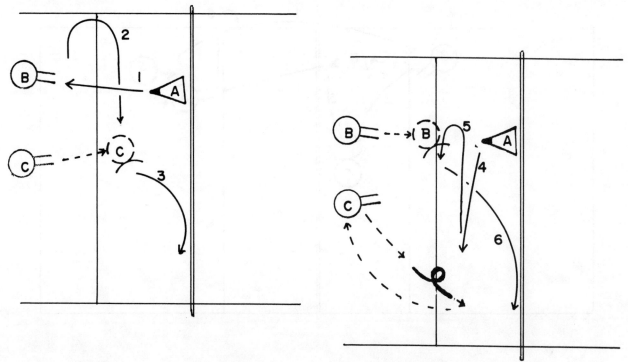

DRILL 222   **DIGGING, DIVING OR ROLLING**   **6 PLAYERS, 15 BALLS**

Player A stands on a table on one side of the net and hits or tips a ball to players B and C. Players B and C take turns diving and digging the balls up as rapidly as possible. Three other players gather balls and feed them to A. Player A should force B and C to move in all directions.

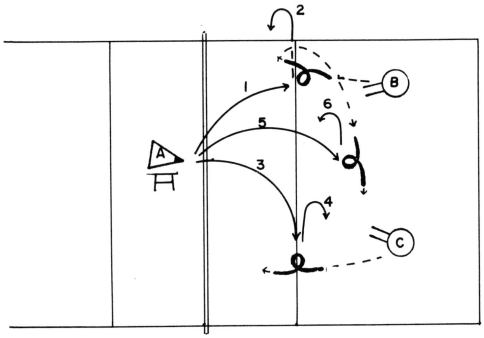

DRILL 223   **PASSING, SETTING, SPIKING, DIGGING**   **3 PLAYERS, 5–10 BALLS**

Player A throws or serves the ball to player B and B passes to C. Player C sets for B to spike and B spikes directly at A. Player A digs the ball and then throws the next ball to B and the sequence is repeated. Practice this drill with different types of sets and passes.

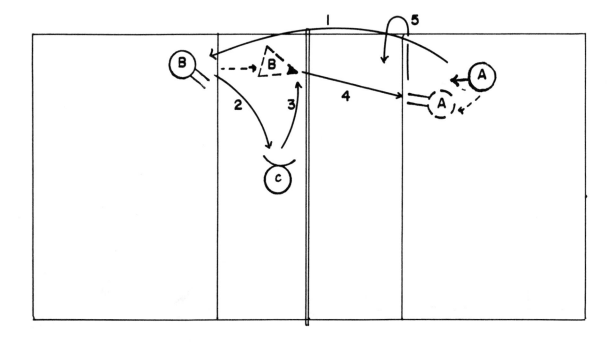

DRILL 224 **SPIKING, DIGGING, SETTING** **4 PLAYERS, 10 BALLS**

Players C and D assume back court positions on one side of the net. Player A, on the other side of the net, sets the ball deep or 10 feet back from the net and player B spikes the ball directly at either C or D. One of them digs the ball and the other sets the ball to a target. Players C and D must then return quickly to their positions and the drill is repeated rapidly.

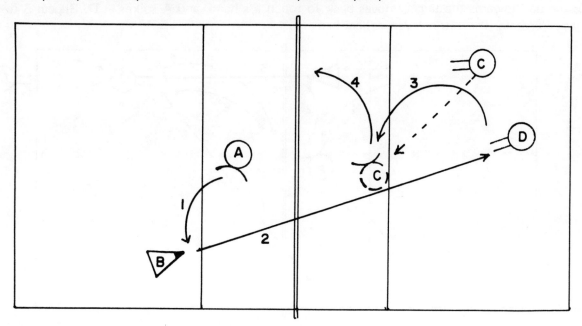

DRILL 225 **SPIKING, DIGGING, SETTING** **4 PLAYERS, 10 BALLS**

Players C and D assume back court positions. Player A throws or sets a ball for B to spike. Player B must hit the ball at half speed directly at C or D. One back court player must dig the ball and the other must run under the ball and set it to a target. Both C and D must then run and touch the back line and quickly assume their back court positions. Repeat the sequence rapidly.

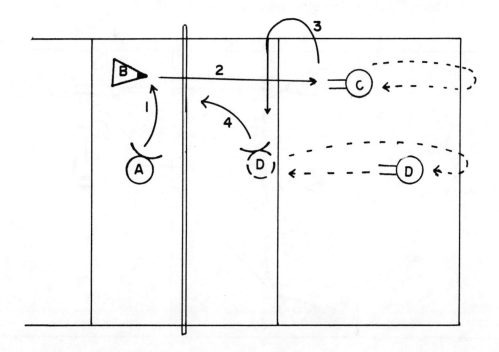

DRILL 226   DIGGING, SPIKING, SETTING   5—7 PLAYERS, 10—20 BALLS

Players A and C spike from each side-line while B sets. Player D starts in a back court position near one side-line. Player A passes to B and B sets for A to spike or tip down the line at D. Player D must dig the ball towards a specified target, move back and touch E's hand, and return to the back court position. Player C then passes to B and B sets for C to spike or tip down the angle at D. Player D digs the ball towards the target, moves back to touch E's hand, and A spikes at D. Repeat 3 to 5 times and rotate. The extra players collect balls.

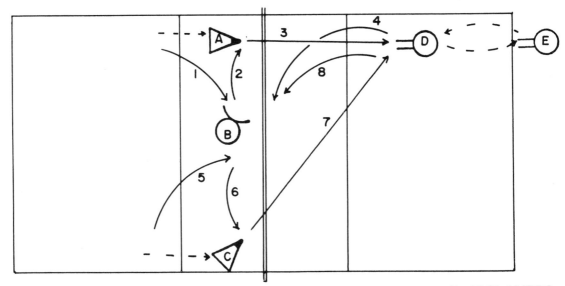

DRILL 227   DIGGING, DIVING AND ROLLING, SPIKING

7—10 PLAYERS, 10—20 BALLS

Player A throws or sets balls alternately to B, C and D on one side of the net. Players B, C and D must spike directly at E who is in one of the back court positions on the other side of the net. After digging each spike, E must run to the back line and touch F's hand and return to dig the next spiked ball. After the third ball has been hit, A throws a ball over the net forcing E to dive or roll to dig the ball. Player F then takes E's place. The other players collect balls for A.

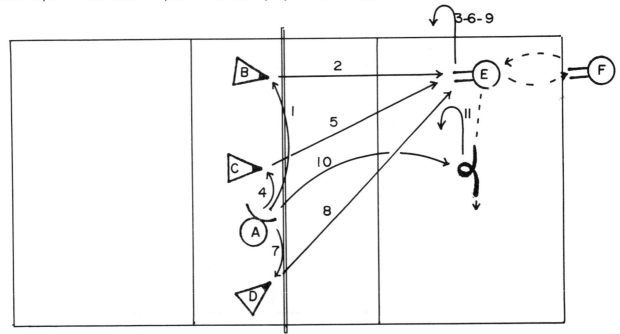

Two players stand on tables close to the net and block. Three players start on the other side of the net and 5 to 10 feet away from the net. The coach hits balls into the blockers' hands and the three players attempt to dig or set the blocked balls.

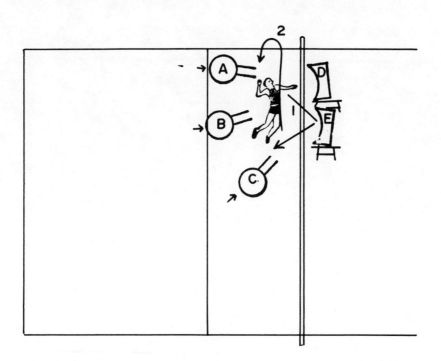

CHAPTER NINE
GAME SEQUENCE DRILLS

Volleyball is a moving game and each player must move to do his part and be ready every time the ball is played. It is important, therefore, that the players be trained in the possible sequences that might occur in a game. After a player has passed the ball, his next play might be spiking, or recovering a blocked ball. After a plyer has served, his next play might be digging a hard spike or diving to recover a tip. This drills in this chapter are designed so that one player will repeat the sequences as they might occur in a game. The skills involved in these sequences are listed in order in the caption for each drill. Try to keep the tempo game-like when doing each drill.

Player A serves to B and A then moves into court. Player B passes the ball to a specified target.
Player C then throws a ball up and player D spikes the ball directly at A. Player A attempts to dig
the ball. Repeat the sequence rapidly. A fifth player returns the balls to A and C. Rotate positions
after 10 serves.

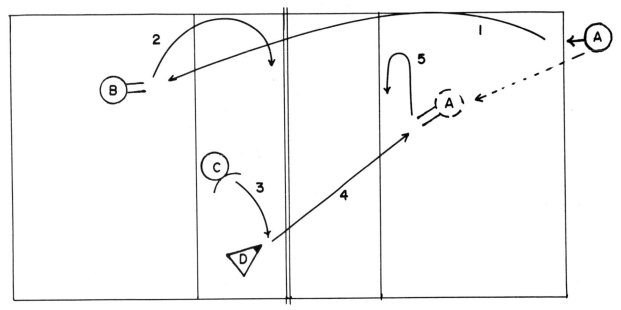

DRILL 230   GAME SEQUENCE — SERVING, DIGGING   5—6 PLAYERS,
                                                                 5—10 BALLS

This drill is similar to the previous drill. Player A serves to B and moves into court. B passes to C
and C sets to D. Player D spikes directly at A. If the ball is poorly passed by B, a fifth player or the
coach throws a ball to C to keep the sequence moving. A sixth player returns the balls to A. Rotate
after 10 serves.

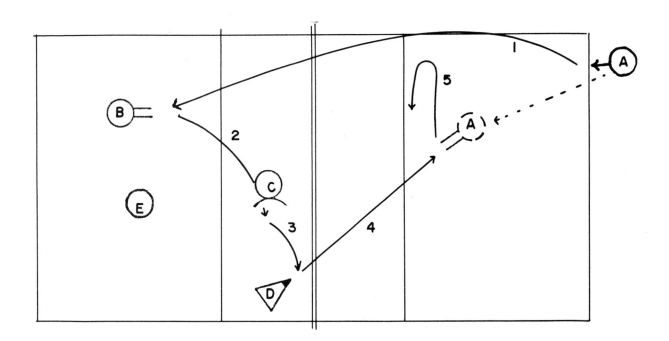

DRILL 231 GAME SEQUENCE – SERVING, DIGGING, COVERING, SETTING 8 PLAYERS, 10–20 BALLS

Player A serves to B and B passes to C. Player C sets to D and D spikes at A. Player A attempts to dig the ball to E and E sets to F. Player F tips the ball to B while A and E move to cover F. Player B passes to C and C sets to D. Player D tips to A and A sets the ball for E to spike. A seventh player or coach is ready to throw in a new ball if the sequence is broken by a bad play. An eighth player collects and returns the balls. Rotate after 10 serves.

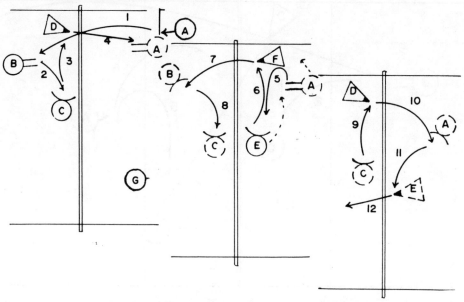

DRILL 232 GAME SEQUENCE – SERVING, SETTING 5–6 PLAYERS, 5–10 BALLS

Player A serves to B and then moves into court. Player B passes the ball to a specified target. Player C then throws a ball up and D tips the ball towards A. Player A moves under the ball and sets to a specified target. Repeat the drill. A fifth player returns balls to A and C.

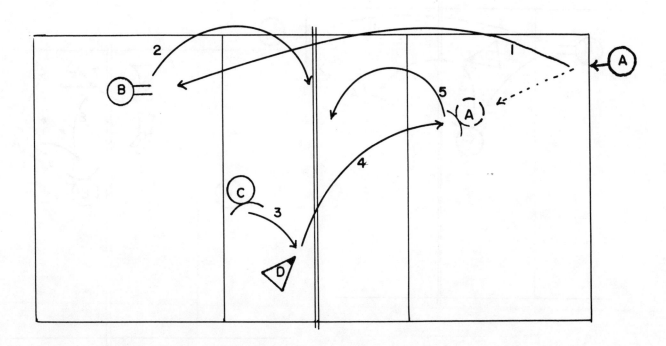

GAME SEQUENCE — SERVING, SETTING 6 PLAYERS, 5—10 BALLS

Player A serves to B and B passes to C. Player C sets to D and D spikes at E. Player E digs the ball and A attempts to set the ball to a specified target. A sixth player returns the balls to A. In case of a bad pass by B, player D should have a ball ready to throw to C to keep the drill going. Player D discards the extra ball if there is a good pass. It may also be necessary to add a seventh player to throw a ball up for A to set if E does not dig the spiked ball.

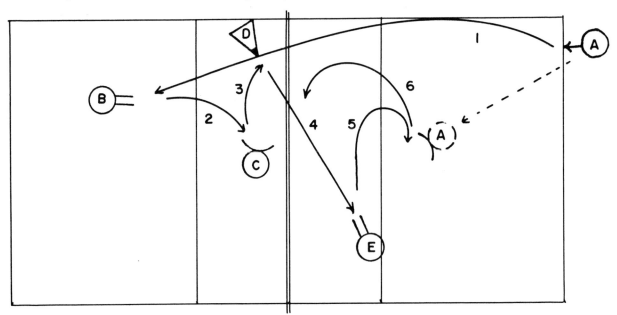

DRILL 234   GAME SEQUENCE — SERVING, PASSING, COVERING   8 PLAYERS, 10—20 BALLS

Player A serves to B. Player B passes to C and C sets to D. Player D tips to A. Player A passes to E and E sets to F. Player F spikes the ball and C and D attempt to block. A and E move to cover F. A seventh player or coach is ready to throw in a new ball if the sequence is broken by a bad play. An eighth player returns the balls.

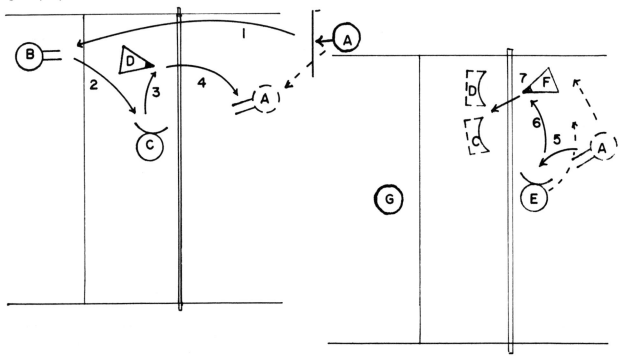

Player A serves to B and B passes to C. Player C sets and B spikes the ball at a specified target. Rotate after 10 serves. A fourth player may be used in receiving thus having two players receiving and spiking.

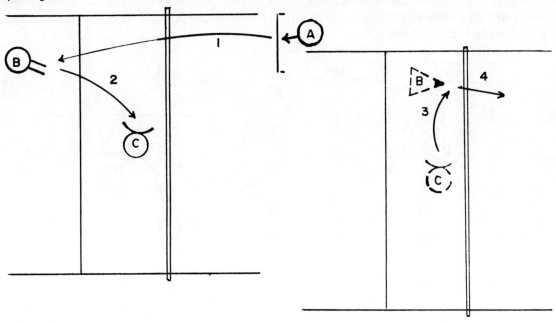

Player A serves to B and B passes to C. Player C sets to B and B spikes the ball at a specified target. Player D then passes a new ball to E and E sets for D to spike. Players B and C attempt to block.

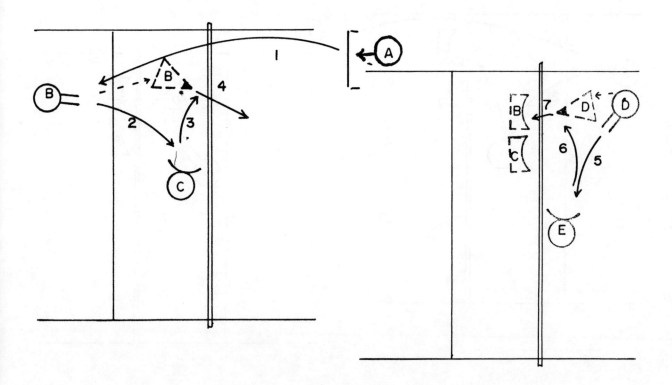

DRILL 237 GAME SEQUENCE — RECEIVING, HITTING, BLOCKING, HITTING

7–8 PLAYERS,
10–20 BALLS

Player A serves to B and B passes to C. Player C sets for B to spike and B spikes at a designated target. Player D then throws a new ball to E and E sets for D to spike while B and C block. Player F then throws or sets a new ball for B to spike while D and E block. Keep the timing gamelike. An eighth player collects and returns balls.

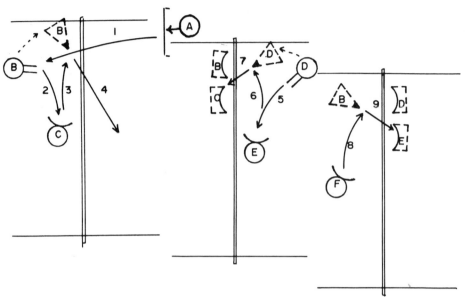

DRILL 238 GAME SEQUENCE — RECEIVING, COVERING

6 PLAYERS,
5–10 BALLS

Player A serves to B and B passes to C. Player C sets for D to spike while E and F block. Players B and C must move to cover the spiker.

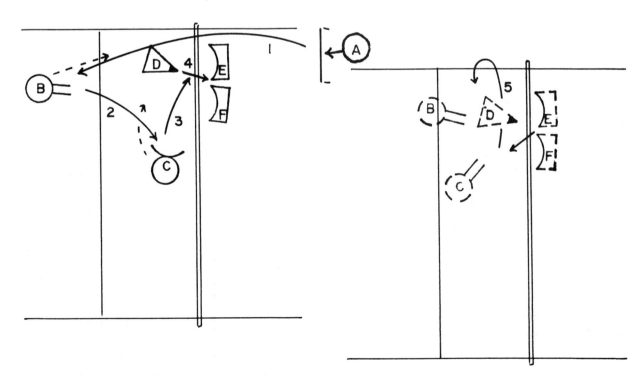

DRILL 239　　**GAME SEQUENCE – RECEIVING, COVERING, PASSING**　　6–7 PLAYERS, 10–20 BALLS

Player A serves to B and B passes to C. Player C sets for D to spike while E and F block. If the ball is blocked, B, C and D attempt to spike again. As soon as the ball passes over the net, A throws a new ball to E and E sets for F. Player F tips the ball towards B and B must pass or set the ball to C. A seventh player collects and returns balls. To modify the drill have A throw the new ball directly to B or have E tip to B.

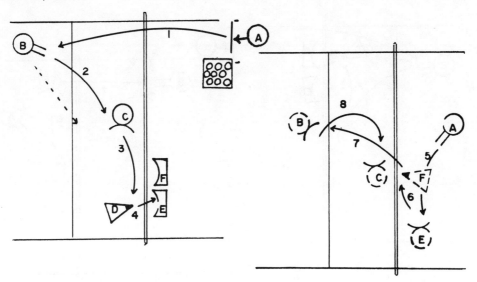

DRILL 240　　**GAME SEQUENCE – RECEIVING, COVERING, SETTING**　　8–9 PLAYERS, 10–20 BALLS

Player A serves to B (or G) and B passes to C. Player C sets to D while E and F block. Player D deliberately hits into the block (or blocking board). Players B, C and G must move to cover D and dig the ball up. Player B attempts to set the recovered ball for D to spike again. If B recovers the ball then G attempts to set. A ninth player collects and returns balls.

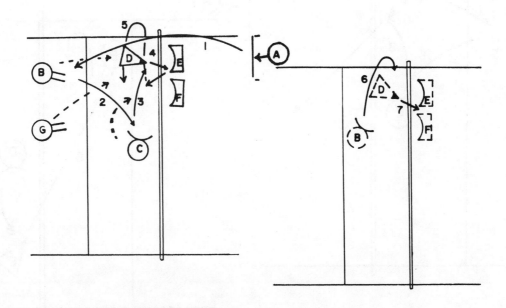

DRILL 241   GAME SEQUENCE — RECEIVING, COVERING, DIGGING   6–7 PLAYERS, 10–20 BALLS

Player A serves to B and B passes to C. Player C sets to D while E and F block. Players B and C must move to cover D. If the ball is blocked, B, C and D attempt to repeat the spiking sequence. As soon as the ball passes over the net, A throws a new ball to E and E sets for F to spike. Player F spikes directly at B. Player B attempts to dig the ball. A seventh player collects and returns balls.

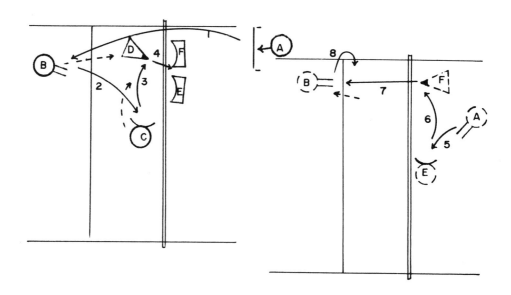

DRILL 242   GAME SEQUENCE — RECEIVING, HITTING, DIGGING   5–6 PLAYERS, 10–20 BALLS

Player A serves to B and B passes to C. Player C sets and B spikes at a specified target. Player A then throws a new ball to D and D sets for E. Player E spikes directly at B and B attempts to dig the ball. A sixth player collects and returns balls.

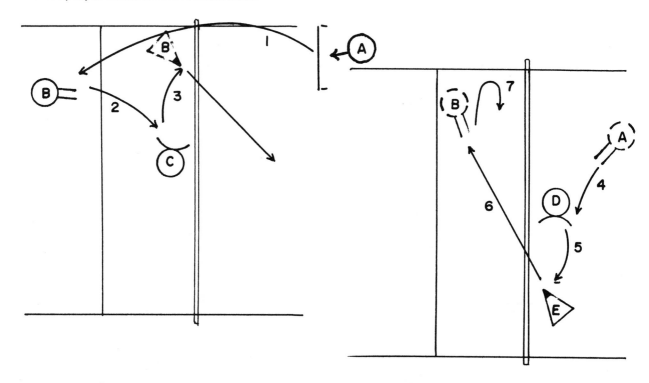

DRILL 243   GAME SEQUENCE — RECEIVING, HITTING, BLOCKING, SETTING

6—7 PLAYERS,
10—20 BALLS

Player A serves to B and B passes to C. Player C sets for B to spike. As soon as B spikes, F throws a new ball to E and E sets for D to spike. Players B and C block. Player F throws a new ball up for B to move under and set to C. Keep the timing and placement of the thrown balls game like. A seventh player collects and returns balls.

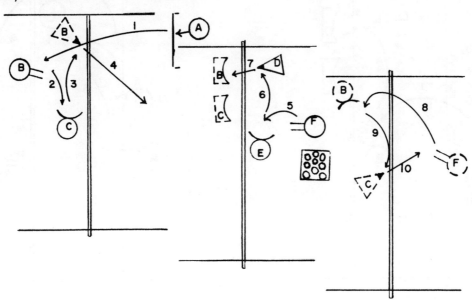

DRILL 244   **GAME SEQUENCE - SETTING, COVERING**   5—6 PLAYERS,
10—20 BALLS

Two players, A and B, alternate setting. Two players, C and D, alternate spiking. A fifth player, E, throws the ball and A sets for C to spike. A moves to cover. Player E then throws a ball and B sets for D to spike. Player B moves to cover. A sixth player returns balls.

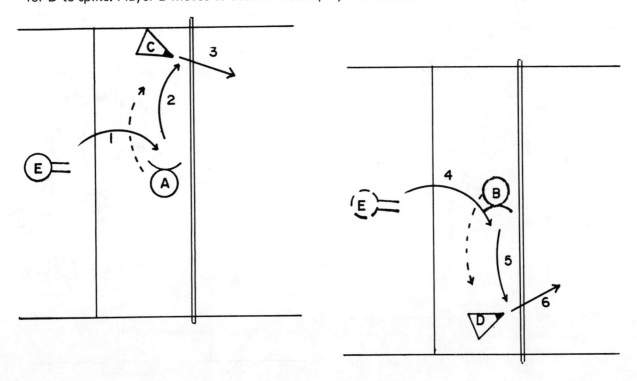

145

DRILL 245   GAME SEQUENCE — SETTING, COVERING, PASSING   6—7 PLAYERS, 10—20 BALLS

Player A throws a ball and B sets for C to spike. Player B moves to cover while D and E block. Player F then throws a ball high and B moves under the ball and passes it to C. Player C passes to A and A starts the sequence again. A seventh player returns balls.

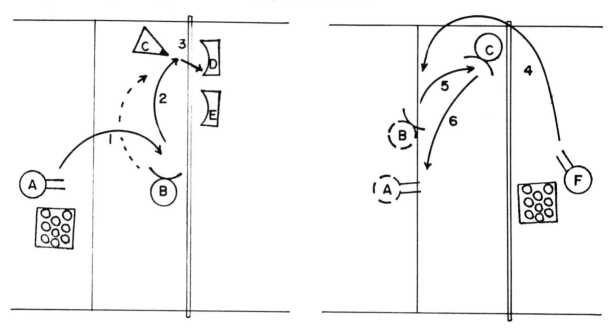

DRILL 246   GAME SEQUENCE — SETTING, COVERING, BLOCKING   6—8 PLAYERS, 10—20 BALLS

Player A throws a ball and B sets for C to spike. B moves to cover while E and F block. D then throws a new ball and E sets for F to spike. Player E moves to cover while B and C block. Repeat the sequence. A seventh and eighth player can return balls.

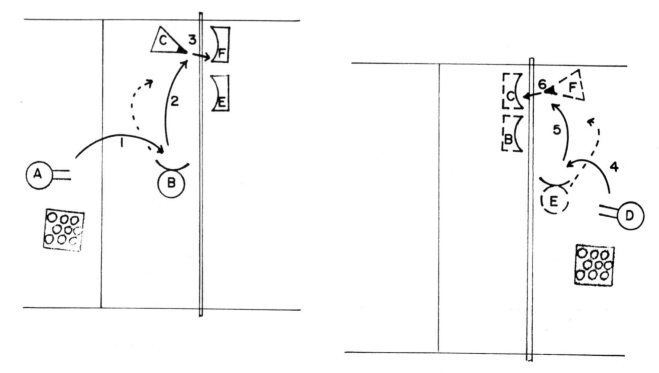

DRILL 247 GAME SEQUENCE — SETTING, COVERING, BLOCKING, SPIKING

**6—7 PLAYERS,
10—20 BALLS**

Player A throws a ball and B sets for C to spike. Player B moves to cover while D and E block. Player F then throws a ball for either D or E to spike while B and C block. Player A then throws a ball to C and C sets for B to spike. A seventh player returns balls.

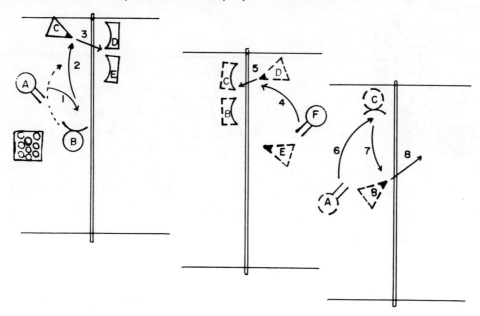

DRILL 248 GAME SEQUENCE - SETTING, COVERING, BLOCKING, BLOCKING

**6—7 PLAYERS,
10—20 BALLS**

Player A throws a ball and B sets for C to spike. Player B moves to cover while D and E block. Player F then throws a ball for E to spike and B and C block. Player F then throws another ball for D to spike and B and C block again. A seventh player returns balls.

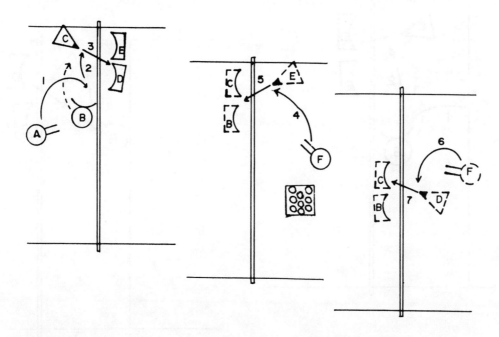

DRILL 249   GAME SEQUENCE — SETTING, COVERING, BLOCKING, SETTING

6—7 PLAYERS,
10—20 BALLS

Player A throws a ball and D sets for C to spike. Player B moves to cover while D and E block. Player F then throws a ball for D to set and E spikes while B and C block. Player A then throws a ball for B to set and C spikes. Continue the sequence. Player D may also move to cover. A seventh player returns balls.

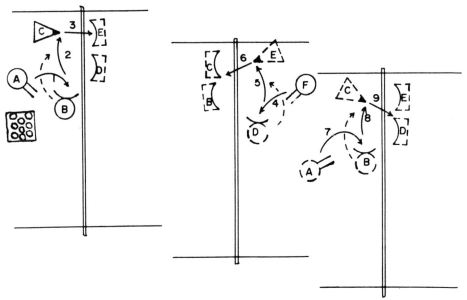

DRILL 250   GAME SEQUENCE — SETTING, COVERING, DIGGING   5—6 PLAYERS,
10 BALLS

Player A throws a ball to B and B sets for C to spike. Players D and E block and C deliberately hits into the block. Players A and B move to dig or recover the blocked ball. Keep playing the ball until it is dead. A sixth player returns the balls.

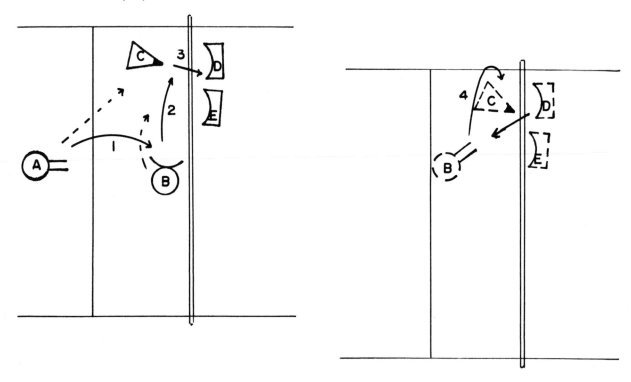

DRILL 251   GAME SEQUENCE - SETTING, SPIKING   4–5 PLAYERS, 10–20 BALLS

Player A throws a ball and B sets for C to spike. Player D then throws a ball up simulating a ball that was blocked or bumped up over the net and B spikes. A fifth player returns balls.

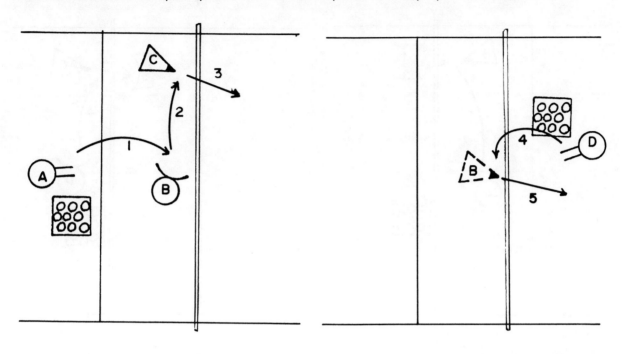

DRILL 252   GAME SEQUENCE — SETTING, SPIKING   3–4 PLAYERS, 10–20 BALLS

Player A throws a ball and B sets for C to spike. Player A then throws a ball and C sets for B to spike. Continue. A fourth player returns balls.

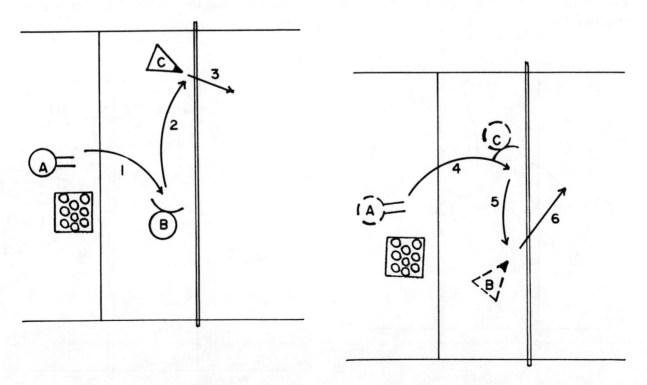

DRILL 253   **GAME SEQUENCE — SPIKING, BLOCKING**

4—5 PLAYERS, 10—20 BALLS

Player A sets a ball for B to spike while C blocks. Player D then throws a ball for C to spike while B blocks. Repeat the sequence. A fifth player returns balls.

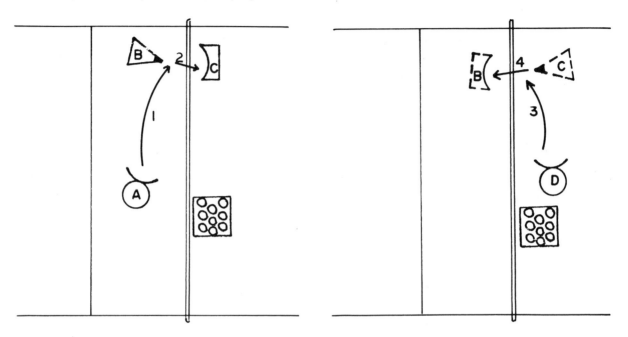

DRILL 254   **GAME SEQUENCE — SPIKING, BLOCKING, SETTING**   6—7 PLAYERS, 10—20 BALLS

Player A throws a ball to B and B sets for C to spike while D blocks. Player E then throws a ball for F to set and D spikes while C blocks. If the ball is successfully blocked, then E throws a ball over thy net for C to set. If D's spike is not blocked, then A throws a ball for C to set. A seventh player returns balls.

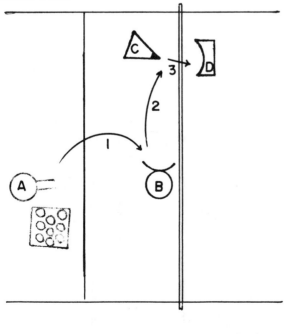
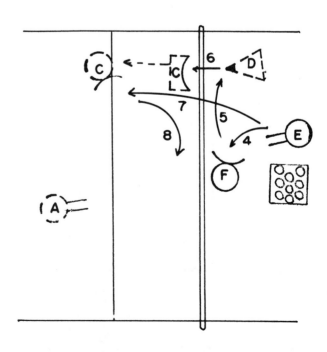

DRILL 255   GAME SEQUENCE — SPIKING, BLOCKING, DIGGING   8—10 PLAYERS, 20 BALLS, 2 TABLES

Player A throws a ball to B and B sets for C to spike while D blocks. Player E then throws a ball to F to set for D to spike while C blocks. Player G, standing on a table, then hits a ball at C and C attempts to dig the ball. Player H hands balls to G and two other players return balls.

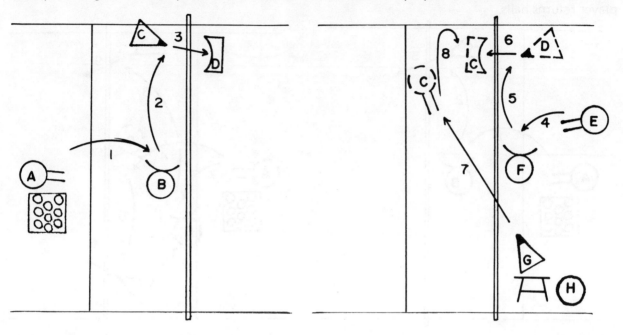

DRILL 256   GAME SEQUENCE — SPIKING, SPIKING   4—5 PLAYERS, 10—20 BALLS

Player A passes to B AND B sets for A to spike. Player C then throws a ball simulating a bumped ball so that A must jump and spike again. Player D then takes A's place and repeats the sequence. A fifth player returns balls.

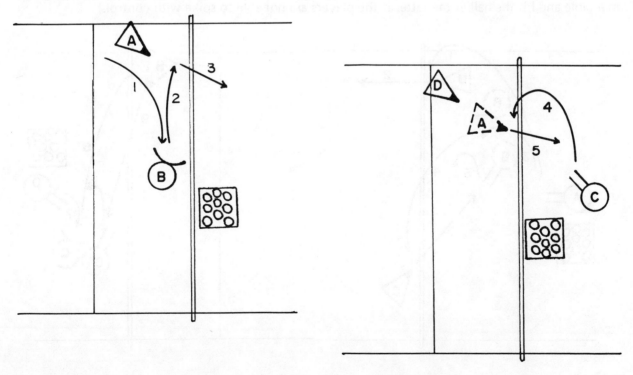

Player A throws a ball to B and B sets for C to spike. Player A then throws a ball to C and C sets for D to spike. Player A then throws a ball to D and D sets for E to spike. Repeat the sequence. The balls may be thrown to different places to force the spiker to move before setting the ball. A sixth player returns balls.

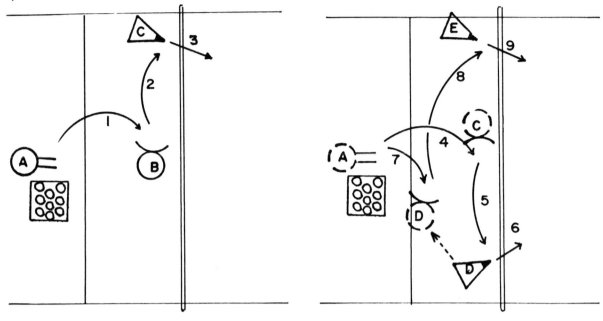

**DRILL 258   GAME SEQUENCE — SPIKING, SETTING, DIGGING   4—6 PLAYERS,
10—20 BALLS**

Player A sets a ball for B to spike. Player A throws a second ball and B sets over the net for C to spike. Player C spikes at B and B digs the ball. Player D then throws a ball for C to set and C sets over the net for B to spike at C. Repeat the sequence. (It may be necessary for the coach to stand on a table and hit the ball at the setter if the players are not able to spike with control.)

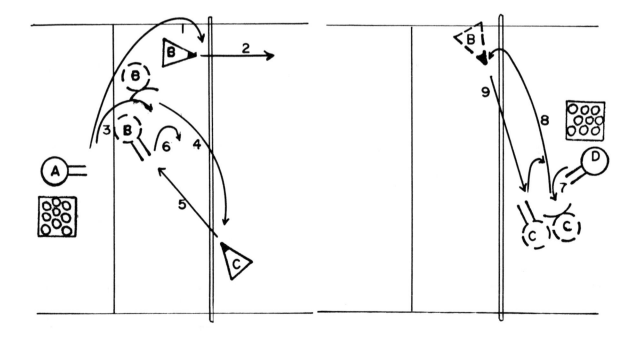

Player A passes to B and B sets for C to spike while D and E block. Player A then throws a ball to B and B sets for F to spike while D and E block. Repeat the sequence. A seventh player returns balls.

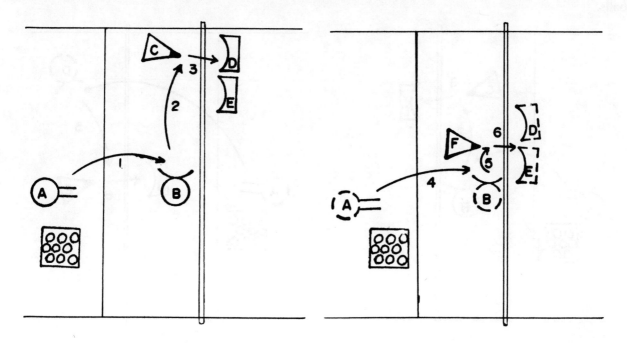

DRILL 260   **GAME SEQUENCE – BLOCKING, NET RECOVERY**   4–5 PLAYERS,
10–20 BALLS

Player A throws a ball over the net to B and B passes to C. Player C sets for B to spike while D blocks. Player A then throws a ball into the net beside D and D digs the ball. A fifth player returns balls.

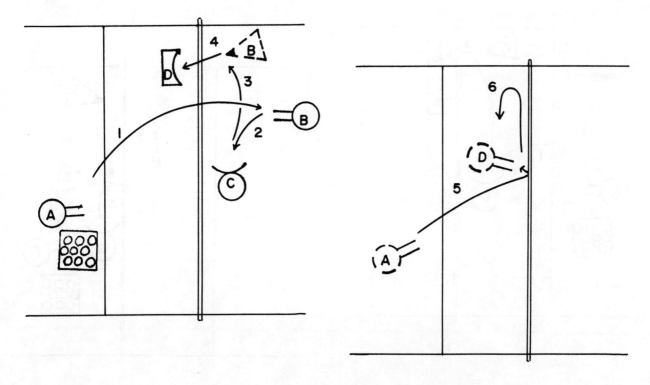

GAME SEQUENCE — BLOCKING, SETTING 5—6 PLAYERS,
10—20 BALLS

Player A throws a ball to B and B sets for C to spike while D blocks. Player A then throws a ball over the net for D to set for E to spike while B blocks. Repeat the sequence. A sixth player returns balls.

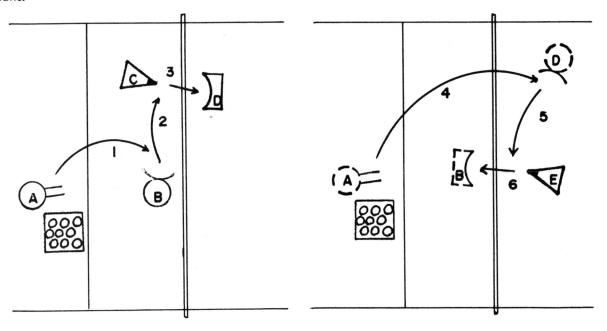

DRILL 262 GAME SEQUENCE — BLOCKING, SPIKING 8—10 PLAYERS,
10—20 BALLS

Player A throws a ball to B and B sets for C to spike while D and E block. Player F then throws a ball to G and G sets for either D or E to spike while C and H block. Repeat the sequence with H spiking at first. Two more players return balls.

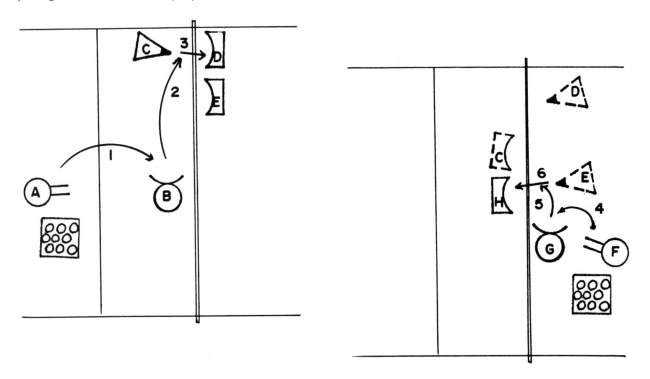

DRILL 263   **GAME SEQUENCE – BLOCKING, SPIKING, SETTING**   6–8 PLAYERS,
10–20 BALLS

Player A passes to B and B sets for C to spike while D and E block. Player A then throws a ball over the net to F and F passes to E and E sets for D to spike while B and C block. Player A then throws a ball over the net and D sets for F to spike while B and C block. Two other players return balls.

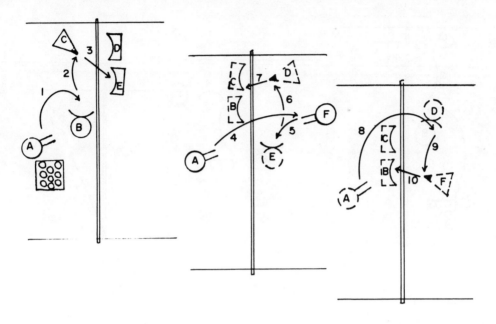

DRILL 264   **GAME SEQUENCE – BLOCKING, SPIKING, DIGGING**   7–9 PLAYERS,
10–20 BALLS

Player A passes to B and B sets for C to spike while D and F block. Player E then throws a ball to F and F sets for D to spike while B and C block. Player A then throws a ball to B and B sets for G to spike. Player G spikes directly at D and D attempts to dig the ball. Two other players return balls.

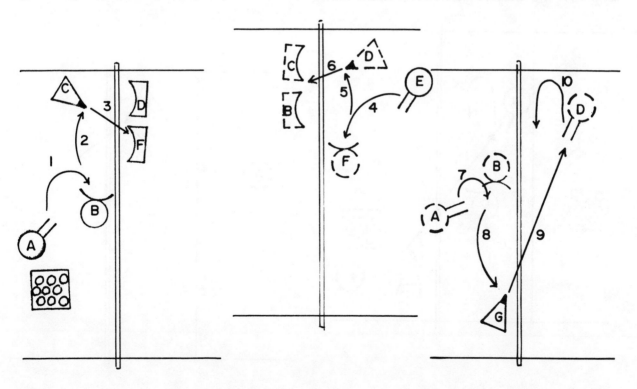

Player A throws a ball to B and B sets for C to spike while D blocks. Player E then throws a ball up for D to set and F spikes. Player G, standing on a table, spikes a ball at D and D attempts to dig the ball. Player A hands balls to G. Two other players return balls.

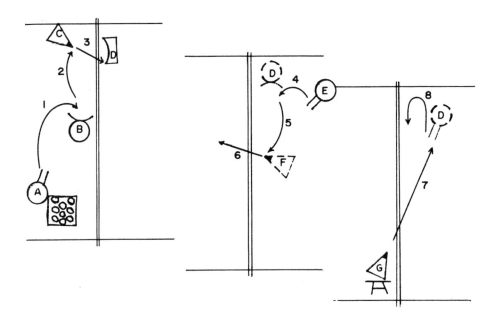

Player A, standing on a table, spikes a ball at B and B digs the ball, so that C can set. If the ball is mishandled, then D throws a new ball to C and C sets for B to spike at a specified target. Player E supplies A with balls. A sixth player returns balls.

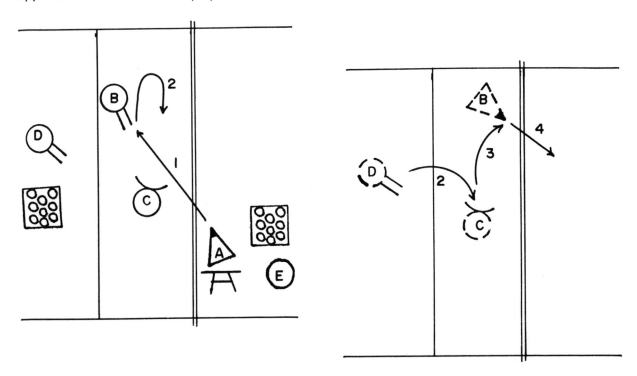

Player A, standing on a table, spikes a ball at B and B digs the ball. Player C moves under the ball and sets for B to spike. Player A then throws a ball behind B and B sets the ball for C to spike. Player D provides A with balls. Two other players return balls.

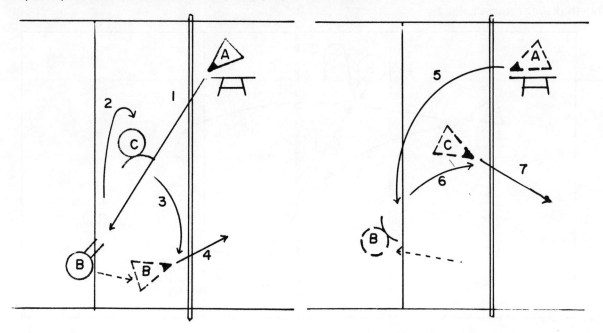

Player A, standing on a table, spikes a ball at B and B digs the ball. Player C then sets or throws a ball for D to spike while B blocks. Player C then sets or throws a ball over the net for B to spike while D blocks. Player E provides A and C with balls. A sixth player returns balls.

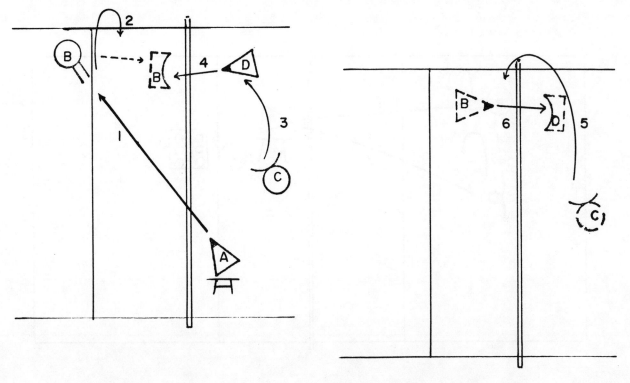

DRILL 269   **GAME SEQUENCE — DIGGING, EMERGENCY ATTACK**   **3–4 PLAYERS**
10–20 BALLS, 1 TABLE

Player A, standing on a table, spikes a ball at B and B digs the ball. Player A then throws a ball forcing B to move to make an emergency play or attack on the ball. Player B attempts to play the ball over the net using either a forearm pass or a standing spike. Player C supplies A with balls. A fourth player returns balls.

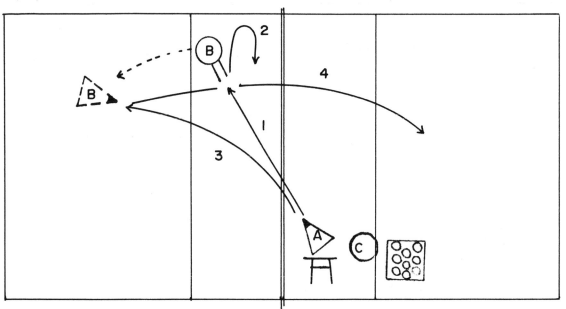

DRILL 270   **GAME SEQUENCE — DIGGING, DIVING OR ROLLING**   **3–4 PLAYERS**
10–20 BALLS, 1 TABLE

Player A, standing on a table, spikes a ball at B and B digs the ball. Player A then throws a second ball to the side of B forcing him to roll, or in front of B forcing him to dive. Player C supplies A with balls. A fourth player returns balls.

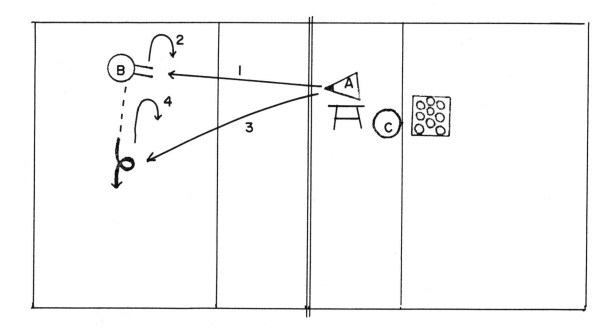

CHAPTER TEN
MODIFIED GAMES AND COACHING IDEAS

Play and competition are universal phenomena and the sample of games presented in this chapter are presented with a view to helping the teacher or coach capitalize on these ready made motivators. It is anticipated that the coach will be stimulated to invent many more games involving volleyball skills. The coaching and practice ideas should also prove to be of interest and assistance to both teachers and coaches. The nucleus of the idea has been presented. The coach will have to build on that nucleus.

DRILL 271   **GAME**   1 PLAYER, 1 BALL

The player passes the ball above his head alternately using a face pass and a forearm pass. Repeat the drill until an error is made or until 50 consecutive passes have been made. Repeat this 4 times and keep score for the maximum number of passes made out of a possible maximum of 200. The player must stop each time he makes a mistake. This test has been used by Jim Coleman to assess passing ability.

DRILL 272   **GAME**   TEAM OR CLASS, 10–20 BALLS,
                                                              4–10 CHAIRS

Spread the chairs around the court on each side of the net. Divide the group into teams. Have the teams serve to the targets. The first team to hit all of the targets is the winner. The teams could also serve to one target and the first team to hit the target 10 times is the winner.

DRILL 273   **GAME**   TEAM OR CLASS, 10 BALLS

Mark a spiking target on the floor as indicated using tape or ropes. One player either throws or sets the balls to the middle of the net and the others spike 10 consecutive balls toward the target. Keep score out of a possible 100 points. Allow the player to repeat any 'bad set'.

DRILL 274   **GAME**   4–40 PLAYERS, 2–20 BALLS

Form teams and run relay races using either a face pass or a forearm pass. You may pass to yourself or pass with a partner.

DRILL 275 GAME TEAM OR CLASS, 15—30 BALLS

Form teams of 3 or more players, Player A starts on one side of the gym and player B starts about 10 feet in front of him. Player B has 3 balls. Player B moves backwards across the gym and throws the balls in front of A forcing A to dive or roll three times. Player C or the other players on the team collect the three balls and B now takes A's place and C throws the balls for B. Player A or the other players on the team again collect the three balls and C takes the diving or rolling position. This relay race should only be done with experienced players.

DRILL 276 GAME 3 PLAYERS, 1 BALL

Play 'monkey in the middle'. Two players start 15 feet apart and pass the ball back and forth. A third player attempts to intercept the pass by blocking. The person who last passed the ball before it was blocked becomes the monkey.

DRILL 277 GAME 4 PLAYERS, 1 BALL

Mark a square on the floor with corners about 15 to 20 feet apart. Three outside players start in 3 of the 4 corners. One player starts as the 'monkey in the middle'. The ball must be passed along the sides of the square in either direction. The outside players must always move to be at right angles to the person who has the ball. The monkey tries to intercept the pass. The player who last passed the ball before it was intercepted becomes the monkey.

DRILL 278 GAME 6—8 PLAYERS, 1 BALL

Five or more players form a circle with another player in the middle of the circle. The outside players pass the ball around the circle in any direction. The middle player may either attempt to block the pass or touch the player before he completes the pass. The passer then takes the middle position.

DRILL 279   **GAME**   6 PLAYERS, 1 BALL

Five players form a circle with a sixth player in the middle of the circle. The ball is passed around the circle in any direction and the middle player must always turn to face the ball. A signal is given and the next person to play the ball must throw or hit the ball at the player in the middle. The middle player attempts to dig the ball up high. If he makes a good pass he stays in the middle. If he makes a poor pass or misses the ball, the next player takes his turn in the middle. The object is to stay in the middle.

DRILL 280   **GAME**   2 PLAYERS, 1 BALL, WALL

Mark a line on the wall 5 feet above the floor and 10 feet long. One player serves to the wall to start the game. The players then alternate passing the ball to the wall above the line. They may use either a face pass or a forearm pass. Use a sideout rule for scoring.

DRILL 281   **GAME**   2 OR MORE PLAYERS, 1 BALL

Mark a hop scotch playing surface on the wall. The players must pass to each area or serve to each area as they would in the normal game of hop scotch.

DRILL 282   **GAME**   2 PLAYERS, 1 BALL,
                                                            WALL OR HANDBALL COURT

The players alternate spiking the ball to the floor and wall. Use a sideout rule for scoring. If only one wall is used, be sure to restrict the playing area.

DRILL 283   **GAME**   6—8 PLAYERS, 20 BALLS

Player B sets for A and A spikes down the angle from the right side. Player D sets for C and C spikes down the angle from the left side. Player E must attempt to dig A's spike and F must attempt to dig C's spike. Alternate spiking rapidly from each side. The coach could throw balls to the setters. Two other players could collect balls. Score 1 point for a spiked ball that is kept in play, 0 for a ball that is touched, and −1 for a ball that is missed. A game is over when the diggers reach a score of +5 or −5. Rotate from spiking to setting to digging.

DRILL 284   **GAME**   TEAM OR CLASS, 10 BALLS

Divide the group into teams of three players. One team starts serving. The other teams alternate receiving. To earn a point for his team the individual server must; (a) touch the ball before it hits the floor on his side, (b) ace the serve, or (c) have the receiving team hit the ball out of bounds or into the net. The receiving team scores a point when they hit the ball into court without it being touched by the individual server. Change serving teams after each game. (Note. Only one player, the server, attempts to play the ball on his side.)

DRILL 285   **GAME**   2 PLAYERS, 5 BALLS, TUMBLING MAT

One player serves and one player receives. The mat is placed on the floor close to the net. The receiver attempts to pass the ball to the target and scores a point each time he hits the target. The server scores each time the receiver misses. This game can be modified so that a player must score three consecutive points to win a game. The receiver can also score a point each time the server serves out of the area or into the net.

DRILL 286   **GAME**   4 PLAYERS, 1 BALL

Two players are on each team. Allow the ball to bounce once on each side of the net. Use a badminton court with young players. You may also play 'one bounce' volleyball and allow the ball to bounce once between each play. This latter modification is more suited to one player against one player.

DRILL 287   **GAME**   3 PLAYERS, 1 BALL

Divide the court in half from one back line to the other. One player is the setter for each of the other two opponents. The setter must move back and forth under the net as the ball passes over the net. Blocking is not allowed.

DRILL 288   **GAME**   4–6 PLAYERS, 1 BALL

The court is divided in half running from one back line to the other. The players must control their attack in this narrow area.

DRILL 289   **GAME**   6 PLAYERS, 1 BALL

Three players are on each team. The game of 'mini volleyball' can be played on a badminton court. Older players can play on a full size court. One innovation with older players is to have two other teams ready to substitute in for each team every time that team loses the serve. The teams stay on the same side of the net and the score is kept between the two sides.

DRILL 290   **GAME**   7 PLAYERS, 1 BALL

Two teams of three players play a game. A seventh player becomes a blocker for both sides. HHeis the only blocker. He must change sides each time the ball passes over the net. This same game may be played using either two or three blockers. Play a game to seven points and then change the blocker(s).

DRILL 291   **COACHING IDEA**   TEAM OR CLASS

Keep the drills simple until the basic skill is learned. Complicated drills and pressure drills can lead to bad habits and weak basic skills if they are attempted too soon. Move on to more complex drills and game-like situations as soon as the players are ready. Too much time spent on basic drills can result in static behavior.

DRILL 292   **COACHING IDEA**   TEAM OR CLASS

Young players and beginning players have some difficulty in adjusting to the speed of the ball. They require more time to move into position to play the ball properly. Allow the ball to bounce once in games and in certain basic drills. This will give the child enough time to move under the ball.

DRILL 293   **COACHING IDEA**   TEAM OR CLASS

Use the time available to optimum advantage. Do not waste time with players standing in line waiting for their turn. Use as many teaching stations as possible and keep the activity ratio as close to 1 on 1 as possible. Players learn by doing and not by waiting in line. Ask how many times each player touched or played a ball during the class or practice.

DRILL 294   **COACHING IDEA**   TEAM OR CLASS

Coach or teacher centered drills are of significant importance. They should be used wisely. The coach must develop the skills in serving, passing, throwing, setting and hitting that are required in order to do these drills. Many of the drills in this book can be adapted.

DRILL 295   **COACHING IDEA**   TEAM OR CLASS

Show the class a list of the skills that can be learned. They can then move on to learn more than the basic skills. A check-off chart posted in the gym is an ideal motivational device.

DRILL 296   **PRACTICE IDEA**   TEAM OR CLASS, NET OR ROPE,
                                                      WALL OR CHALK BOARD

Stretch a net or rope at regulation height and 6 to 10 inches away from a wall or chalk board. The player must jump and touch the wall as high as possible without touching the net. Compare the players on their jumping ability.

DRILL 297   **PRACTICE IDEA**   TEAM OR CLASS, 10 BALLS

Mark a target on the court. Have each player serve once to the target. If he misses, everyone must do one push up. Be sure that the size of the target is appropriate for the skill level of the players.

DRILL 298   **PRACTICE IDEA**   TEAM, 30—50 BALLS

Have each member of the team serve a specified number (25—50) of serves consecutively into court before leaving the gym after practice. The player must start after each error.

DRILL 299   **PRACTICE IDEA**   TEAM, 30—50 BALLS

Have each member of the team set a specified number (10—15) of balls into a basketball hoop from the free throw line before leaving the gym after practice.

DRILL 300   **PRACTICE IDEA**   TEAM, ROPE

Stretch a rope across the court about 12 feet above the floor and 6 feet back from the net. The receivers must pass the ball over the rope to the setter.

DRILL 301   **PRACTICE IDEA**   TEAM, 10—20 BALLS

Mark a target on the floor. Have each player in turn either serve to the target or spike at the target. For each miss the team must do 5 serves at the end of practice.

DRILL 302   **PRACTICE IDEA**   TEAM OR CLASS, 20—30 BALLS

Introduce two and three player games that the team members or class members can play before the practice or class starts. These games should be vigorous and result in fun and a general warm up. Some games have been included in the section of this book on games.

DRILL 303   COACHING IDEA   TEAM OR CLASS

Keep the ball in play until it hits the floor. Allow four or more plays on one side of the net during certain drills or games. Work on the concept that the ball is not dead until it hits the floor.

DRILL 304   COACHING IDEA   TEAM OR CLASS

Teach the players how to chase and collect balls. Very often much time is wasted chasing balls. This time period could be used for conditioning. Be sure that the players are always on the run.

DRILL 305   COACHING IDEA   TEAM OR CLASS

Never hold or catch a ball. Have the players pass or bump the ball to themselves rather than catching or holding the ball. When they are standing in line have them pass the ball to themselves or bat the ball back and forth between their hands.

DRILL 306   PRACTICE IDEA   TEAM OR CLASS

When performing push ups at any time, have the players simulate the action used in the dive. Have them raise one leg high and rock into the push up.

DRILL 307   **COACHING IDEA**   TEAM OR CLASS

It is wise to use padding on the more vulnerable parts of the body when learning and practicing dives and rolls. Towels or foam can be used to protect the hip area. Knee pads and elbow pads can be used. Tumbling mats should also be used to help build confidence.

DRILL 308   **PRACTICE IDEA**   TEAM, CANDY

Have the spikers or servers aim at a target. Each time they hit the target they win a prize. Jelly beans make excellent prizes. This drill or idea can also be used in tipping toward a target.

DRILL 309   **PRACTICE IDEA**   TEAM

The team can agree to certain penalties for making errors during a particular drill. These should normally be in the way of conditioning exercises or extra basic skill drills. These penalties can be performed immediately or they can be totaled and done at the end of the practice. Examples of conditioning exercises would be squat jumps, rolls, jump and touch, push ups. Examples of extra drills might be serving, spiking, or setting to a target.

DRILL 310   **PRACTICE IDEA**   TEAM

Have the spikers work against the blockers, or the servers work against the receivers. Set the game at 5 or 7 points depending upon the skill level of the players. The losers must carry the winners around the gym on their backs. Keep the games short enough so that several games can be completed in a short time.

DRILL 311 COACHING IDEA TEAM OR CLASS

Make drills competitive to add interest and increase motivation. I do not mean competitive in a deadly serious way, but competitive in a fun way. Ask young children, "Who can do 20 passes?". Have groups attempt to serve 25 balls in or to hit a target 15 times.

DRILL 312 COACHING IDEA TEAM OR CLASS

Provide specific goals for the player to reach. He or she then has something concrete to work towards and will generally work much harder. Be sure that the goals are appropriate to the ability level of the player. Examples of specific goals might be: (a) 10 completed passes, (b) 10 consecutive serves without an error, or (c) 4 sequences out of 5.

DRILL 313 COACHING IDEA TEAM

Determine the goals of each player on your team very early in the season. Ask the players what they want to achieve this year and in future in volleyball. Some players simply want to make the team, while others want to win. The coach must understand the player's goals in order to help him achieve those goals and also to avoid conflicts later in the season.

DRILL 314 COACHING IDEA TEAM

Develop a club concept with 2 or more teams in the club. No player likes to sit on the bench. If you have a second team, the substitutes all get a chance to play and will gain experience. They will be that much better when you need them. Most coaches feel that 8 or 9 players on a team is sufficient.

7977

DATE DUE